"'Mom? Why do people die? What is adultery?' As a mother of seven children who range in age from toddler to adult, I'm always interested in grace-filled, Bible-based answers to the tough questions of this life. Elyse and Jessica do a beautiful job of balancing truth with grace, while offering parents practical, solid answers to topics that many parents cringe over. I'll be looking at this great guide again and again, not because it contains all the answers, but because the authors humbly point parents back to the only source of truth that's ever existed: the Bible."

—Heidi St. John, author and speaker

"I love this book! I will recommend it again and again. It is street-level theology for children that drips with the gospel of Jesus Christ. Parents, read it, live with it, share it daily with your children, and not only will they learn and grow, you will, too."

—Paul David Tripp, president, Paul Tripp Ministries

"These hard questions aren't random—children wonder about these issues, and they impact our everyday lives. Now talking about these questions doesn't have to be overwhelming for lack of resources. I'm so thankful for Elyse and Jessica's hard work, precision, and focus on Christ in this book."

—Gloria Furman, author of *Glimpses of Grace*
and *Treasuring Christ When Your Hands Are Full*

"Jessica and Elyse have done it again—offering the good news of the gospel to moms and dads overwhelmed by their inadequacy. This is a scripturally rooted and profoundly wise guide for parents who desire to swers to their kids' toughest qu book. It takes the pressure off pa rs, reveals the radical nature of rlet thread of redemption' throu

—Jeannie Cunnion, MSW, author of *Parenting
the Wholehearted Child*

"Elyse and Jessica have written a must-have book for parents and those involved with ministry to children. It provides helpful, gracious, wise, and faithful answers to some of the most difficult questions children can ask about the Christian faith. My wife and I use this book with our daughters, and we are thankful for the work that went into it and the heart behind it."

—Justin S. Holcomb, Episcopal priest, seminary professor, and coauthor of *Rid of My Disgrace: Hope and Healing for Victims of Sexual Assault* and *Is It My Fault? Hope and Healing for Those Suffering Domestic Violence*

"Martin Luther once said he measured his ability as a preacher by his ability to communicate the gospel to the young. This book is filled with such gospel truth, so simply articulated. No one has helped me connect the gospel to parenting more than Elyse Fitzpatrick and Jessica Thompson."

—J.D. Greear, PhD, author of *Ready to Launch: Jesus-Centered Parenting in a Child-Centered World* and *Stop Asking Jesus Into Your Heart*

"When I have a tough parenting question, Elyse and Jessica are my go-to friends—not because they have it all together, but because I know that their wisdom will be driven by none other than the gospel. This book is just what I need, and it's just what you need, too!"

—Kimm Crandall, mother of four and author of *Christ in the Chaos: How the Gospel Changes Motherhood*

"This is a great book to help answer the big theological questions of little children."

—Pastor Mark Driscoll

Answering Your Kids'
Toughest
Questions

Answering Your Kids'
Toughest Questions

HELPING THEM UNDERSTAND
Loss, Sin, Tragedies, and Other Hard Topics

Elyse Fitzpatrick and Jessica Thompson

BETHANY HOUSE PUBLISHERS
a division of Baker Publishing Group
Minneapolis, Minnesota

© 2014 by Elyse Fitzpatrick and Jessica Thompson

Published by Bethany House Publishers
11400 Hampshire Avenue South
Bloomington, Minnesota 55438
www.bethanyhouse.com

Bethany House Publishers is a division of
Baker Publishing Group, Grand Rapids, Michigan

Printed in the United States of America

Library of Congress Cataloging-in-Publication Data
Fitzpatrick, Elyse.
    Answering your kids' toughest questions : helping them understand loss, sin, tragedies, and other hard topics / Elyse Fitzpatrick & Jessica Thompson.
        pages cm
    Includes bibliographical references.
    Summary: "Helpful information and age-appropriate guidelines for answering kids' toughest questions on difficult topics, including death, violence, evil, and more"— Provided by publisher.
    ISBN 978-0-7642-1187-4 (pbk. : alk. paper))
    1. Parenting—Religious aspects—Christianity. 2. Child rearing—Religious aspects—Christianity. 3. Christian education of children—Miscellanea. 4. Theology, Doctrinal—Miscellanea. I. Title.
BV4529.F557 2014
230—dc23   2014003630

Cover design by Dual Identity

14   15   16   17   18   19   20   7   6   5   4   3   2   1

To all the moms and dads
who are trying to reconcile
the heartache and
brokenness of this world
with what they know
about their loving God.

Elyse

To my gospel community:
Cody, Kei, Wayne, Keri, Mark,
Katie, Anthony, Phoenix, and Derek,
I couldn't have done this without you.
You all taught me what true community
looks like during the process of writing a book.

Jessica

Contents

Introduction

Thank you for taking time to pick up this book and for loving your family the way you do. I know there are plenty of other demands on your time, and reading a book about answering your children's hard questions might not top the list, but your interest tells me that you want to help them as they face daily contradictions, depravity, and destruction around them.

You don't need me to tell you that we live in a world of great suffering and deep rebellion against God. This is the reality today—but it isn't all that different from the world children were born into two thousand years ago in Ephesus, Corinth, and Rome. In fact, in many ways our world isn't as bad as theirs. While we might not be happy about the direction our communities are headed, we do have laws that serve to protect many of us. So take courage. The words of Scripture that brought hope to our ancient brothers and sisters are the same words that can help us as we search for answers today.

Some Answers Before We Really Begin

This Isn't a Script

Although we will emphasize throughout this book that it is not to be used like a script, we want to underscore it here. The importance of knowing each of your children and how to talk to them in language they understand is crucial, especially when you're trying to answer difficult questions. So, while we will suggest ways to discuss each topic (for three different age groups), make sure to speak to your child in his or her own language. In addition, the Holy Spirit may guide your conversation in a completely different direction, and we want you to be open to this. *Again, this isn't a script.*

The Voice Who Will Be Speaking

In the chapters ahead, I (Jessica) will be doing the majority of the speaking. My mother, Elyse, will be helping me think through the tough questions and helping me present them to you. It is more than a little ironic that as I am writing a book on answering kids' questions, my mom is helping me.

Please know this book is not written from an "I have it all together" position, but rather from an "I'm in the same boat as you" perspective. Like you, I am a sinful, dreadfully flawed parent. Like you, I struggle with knowing when and how to talk to my kids about these tough topics. I fail to fight unbelief, and I worry that I don't communicate in an understandable way. I simply pray that you find this book helpful, and that no matter the topic, we parents are able to express Jesus' love for the broken and his beautiful rescue of sinners.

I believe that God is sovereign over everything, including the salvation of souls. I also believe the Bible is inerrant and sufficient: In everything it speaks to, it is correct, and it contains all we need to know about how God loves us and how we are to love him.

My theology will come out in every question I address, but it is not my purpose to be provocative or pushy. So as you work through the different answers, I encourage you to ask yourself what you believe and, as always, to go to the Bible for further understanding and growth.

Each chapter will begin with a basic explanation of the biblical answer to the chapter's question. I'll use Scripture, metaphors, and stories from our lives to flesh out these explanations in a way that, hopefully, clarifies the answer for you, the parent. It's difficult to answer a child's questions—even in simplified, child-friendly language—without deeply understanding the answer ourselves.

From there, each chapter will provide example discussions you can have with your children at three age ranges: preschool, ages five to ten, and ages eleven and up. Finally, each chapter ends with a section called "In a Nutshell," which summarizes the truths presented in the chapter. I have added these helps so that you can go to them when you're in a hurry and need a quick reminder of what the chapter covered.

My Desire for You

Although Christians may disagree on some points of theology, my desire is that every conversation reflects the gospel of Jesus Christ. As Paul wrote, the gospel is of first importance (1 Corinthians 15:3). Our God loves us so much that he sent his one and only Son into the Enemy's camp to die for the very ones who hated him.

Jesus lived in our broken world. He understands the temptation to doubt God's goodness when there is so much sin around us. Christ himself was tempted in every way we are tempted today, yet he did not sin. He lived the life we have been called to live; he died the death we deserved to die. He intercedes for us even now before his Father's throne. God is not some cosmic distant uncle who doesn't care about what happens to us on earth. Indeed, he is aware of every sparrow that falls to the ground (Matthew 10:29). He was and is intimately involved in every event in history. There was never a moment when he was not in control.

God's untamable love goes to the ends of the earth to pursue us sinners. This completely counterintuitive truth is the point of all of life. And because of his great heart, God's love for his children in Christ is the focal point of every discussion we encourage you to have with your kids.

Fellow parent, as you read this book I pray you have hope— hope that God is more powerful than all of our past mistakes, hope that God uses our weaknesses to glorify himself, and a deeper hope that he can speak over and through our faulty, muddled words.

One more thing: At the back of the book is a list of recommended resources for further study. The nature of this book doesn't allow extensive coverage of the topics, so if something piques your interest and you would like to know more, I encourage you to read these helpful books by authors I trust.

1

Parenting Is More Than Room and Board

Parenthood is such a strange thing. For many of us, it seems as though we had barely grown up and, before we knew it, helpless little strangers were relying on us for everything—their needs far exceeded having a place to live and food to eat. With smiles and gentle touches, we were the ones who brought comfort and order into their disordered and oh-so-confusing worlds. Time flew by, and soon *whys?* were coming from our little ones, often met by our own loss for words. *How did we end up on the receiving end of this little bundle full of questions?*

There is one thing you can count on as your children get older: They will have more questions than you will have answers. As Christian comedian Tim Hawkins recently tweeted,

> Anyone who fields spiritual questions from a 7 year old deserves an honorary Masters in Theology. Wow.[1]

How will you answer little Janie when she asks a difficult question? Are you like us, wondering all the time what you're supposed to say? *I'm the parent*, you think. *Aren't I supposed to have the answers?* And then, because you are a Christian, the problem is compounded: *Shouldn't my answers reflect a mature and consistent faith?*

We all know what it feels like to be asked questions we don't know how to answer. Sometimes we try to deflect:

Janie: Mom, what's a homosexual?
Mom: Look, dear, a giraffe.

Other times we make futile efforts to ignore:

Johnny: Daddy, why did Abraham have two wives?
Dad: *[Haunting silence followed by faking a call on his cell phone.]*

At still other times, we respond by blustering and playing the you're-too-young-to-know-that card:

Janie: Mom, why did God allow the devil to live?
Mom: When you're old enough to go to bed without my yelling at you AND when you're old enough to get up in the morning without my having to blow an air horn in your ear AND when you can make your own breakfast AND clean up afterward without complaining, THEN I'll answer that question.

Yes, it seems that we all need master's degrees in theology, not to mention way more patience, wisdom, and insight than Solomon. But the truth is, most of us are still in theological kindergarten. And I'm right there with you.

The alternative many of us choose is the fake-it-till-you-make-it route. We pretend we have all the answers, thinking that if we can just be clever and use big words confidently enough, our children won't guess that we don't know what we're talking about. With just the right amount of smoke and precise placement of mirrors, we'll try to convince them that they should trust us and believe everything we say without question. And when the smoke starts to clear and the crack in the mirror shows up, we think that's the time to pump up the volume. After all, if we're really passionate and convincing in our arguments, our children will find it easy to believe us. There's one problem, though: Most children, like adults, have an innate capacity to see through smoke and mirrors.

We Do Not Have All the Answers . . . and That's Okay

Let's get real. The truth is, no matter how much we pray or study, none of us, not even those of us with real theological degrees, have all the answers. We all struggle with what's known as the noetic effect of sin, which means our ability to know and understand truth is broken, in the same way our bodies are broken. Our thought processes have been affected by sin, too. We simply can't understand deep truth.

But that's not our only problem. We have our own doubts and fears. When we hear about the failure of a friend's marriage or read about a tsunami somewhere in the world, we can wonder if there really is a God who is overseeing this mess—and if he is there, why isn't he doing something about it? We scratch our heads and wonder *why?* just like our children do.

We try to make sense of the Bible, but then we come across stories that are out-and-out strange, or thorny topics that are difficult to understand even as an adult with a well-defined worldview. We try to trust the character of God and what he says about the world around us, but at times it seems to conflict with what we see on the news, in our neighbors' lives, or even in our own hearts. It's so easy to wonder if our lack of faith or confidence about certain biblical matters will harm our children.

It might be hard to believe, but all of this is okay. Quite simply, we are called to walk by faith, not by sight (2 Corinthians 5:7). Yes, it can be disheartening and even frightening when we don't have the answers or the words to explain the truth we know. But as David expressed, God can be trusted:

> When I am afraid, I put my trust in you. In God, whose word I praise, in God I trust; I shall not be afraid.
>
> Psalm 56:3–4

In the past, when my kids asked me questions I couldn't answer, my fear was based on a wrong assumption—that their understanding of God and even their ultimate salvation depended upon my ability to make sense of all the brokenness in the world. I'm thankful that now I truly understand that as good as it is to have answers and to seek to be prepared to speak to my children about my beliefs, their ultimate salvation isn't up to me.

No, the salvation of souls depends on the Lord alone (Psalm 3:8; Jonah 2:9; John 1:12). Our children's salvation is not dependent on the strength of our faith or the shrewdness of our answers. Of course, we are called to bring our children up in the "discipline and instruction of the Lord" (Ephesians 6:4), but our response to this command may or may not be determinative in our children's salvation. Think of it: None of the Gentile believers who came to faith in the early years of the church had been raised in the discipline and instruction of the Lord. They had been raised in Greek philosophy. In fact, even the Jewish Christians, who had been raised in the law of Moses, had to be saved by a sovereign act of the Holy Spirit in their hearts . . .

just like us. Yes, we are to have answers, but no (thankfully!), our answers will not save our children.

We are commanded to train our children—to teach them how to understand and apply truth, even if they resist it (Proverbs 22:6; Deuteronomy 6:7). My parents worked hard to help my brothers and me learn to discern truth from error. For instance, when I was about fifteen, I remember coming home from a movie and finding my mother waiting for me. I admit I was annoyed because I knew what was coming. She was going to challenge me to think about what I had seen and whether the message of the movie was true or false. I remember sitting with her and whining, "It was just a movie, Mom! Do you have to analyze *everything*?" But now I find myself asking my children about movies they see and trying to help them think about truth and error. I want to guide them, to help them discern the difference between what's real and fake. I want them to know that there is only one basis for truth—one rule by which all of life is to be judged. God has given us the Bible, our standard to judge all of life by. And every movie, every conversation, every book, every thought is to be brought into line with what God has told us about the world he created. I want my children to have these answers, whether they are the answers they want or not, whether they make perfect sense to them, or whether they seem strange and completely antithetical to everything they hear from their friends.

There Is True Truth

I want my children to know that truth is outside of them; it doesn't originate with them. It is not subjective or based on thoughts or feelings. There actually is what evangelical Christian theologian Francis Schaeffer used to call "true truth," a truth that transcends what our feelings or our culture or environment tells us is right and wrong, true or false. We live in a world that has been built upon the lie that there is no such thing as objective truth, that what is true for one person may not be true for everyone else. Of course, that statement—there is no truth to be known—is, in itself, a truth statement. And it is false.

Into this subjective world of ever-altering "truths," the Bible stands as a fortress of infallible, unchanging truth. And it is more than a rulebook, more than a list of do's and don'ts. The Bible is God's love letter to his children through which we learn how to interpret and interact with the world around us, and through which we find salvation.

> You have been born again, not of perishable seed but of imperishable, through the living and abiding word of God; for "all flesh is like grass and all its glory like the flower of grass. The grass withers, and the flower falls, but the word of the Lord remains forever." And this word is the good news that was preached to you.
>
> 1 Peter 1:23–25

Yes, we look to the Bible as the guide we need. We seek to understand its meaning, and then we stand in faith that God's Word is true truth. We strive to teach our children to know what it says and teach them all about the good news of the Rescuer who calls himself the truth (John 14:6), and then we rest and pray and wait for that good, "imperishable" seed to take root and grow.

This Truth Will Set You Free

John 6:63 offers so much freedom: "It is the Spirit who gives life." Knowing it is the Holy Spirit's work (not ours) to regenerate hearts frees us to pray that he would work powerfully through both our weaknesses and our strengths. We can seek God for our children, both in extended times of prayer and also in little whispers within our hearts when we sense an opportunity for conversation.

Knowing that salvation is God's work alone should also free us from fear. We no longer have to fear that everything is riding on what we say—that we might miss that "one" opportunity to speak into our children's lives and have their eternal salvation forfeited. Instead, we should feel the freedom to tell them, "I'm not sure . . . let me pray (or think or do some research) on that, and I'll get back to you."

Not being willing to admit that we do not have all the answers actually demonstrates a pride that will get between us and our children. Pretending to be all-knowing makes us seem unapproachable and hypocritical. And while that may cut down on the number of questions we will have to answer, it certainly won't build a relationship. Freedom from fear means we can admit we were wrong, we didn't understand an issue, or we answered in haste.

Freed from fear, we won't need to try to avoid our children's questions. And because we are commanded to speak the truth in love (Ephesians 4:15), we should be asking the Lord for grace and wisdom when we answer. We need wisdom to know how to speak to them in age-appropriate ways. We also need to know them well enough that we are aware of their emotional and spiritual states.

The Rocky Road Ahead

Our children will have questions about what they hear in church or read in the Bible. They will want to know about sin, death, hell, heaven, and the angels. They will also have questions about what they see in the world around them. They'll want to know what rape, incest, homosexuality, and abuse are. They will wonder about natural disasters that bring death and destruction on seemingly innocent people without any obvious purpose. They will want to know why the Bible has such strange stories in it—stories that seem to promote marrying more than one woman, having sex with hundreds of women, crucifying an innocent man, destroying entire cities because of sin, and much more. And they will want to know how God could insist that he's both good and in control of all of this mess.

The questions we'll be discussing in this book are difficult. But even when we feel ill prepared and unsure, we should still attempt the conversation. Perhaps in this weak act of faith and love, we will find the wisdom we need. Perhaps the Lord will open our understanding and give us words to say. Or, he may not. But even at those times, we can trust him. We can trust him because he is good, he is wise, and he is loving.

> For it is you who light my lamp;
> the Lord my God lightens my darkness.
> For by you I can run against a troop,
> and by my God I can leap over a wall.
> This God—his way is perfect;
> the word of the Lord proves true;
> he is a shield for all those who take refuge in him.
>
> Psalm 18:28–30

2

What Is Sin?

What if you were a frog? I know that's quite a leap (smile), but just play along for a moment, if you please. And what if being a frog was against the Law of the Lily Pond?

Well, of course, to avoid getting into trouble you could try to curb all your desires to jump or catch flies with your long, sticky tongue. And every time you felt like you needed to croak, you could try to stifle that urge and sing like a canary instead. You might even glue dragonfly wings on your back or fins on your sides. Still, no matter how you might try to disguise your froggy-ness or change those outward amphibian behaviors, you would remain a frog. . . . And you would still be in trouble. That's because the Law of the Lily Pond does not prohibit jumping or croaking or munching on bugs. The Law of the Lily Pond prohibits frogs. Your problem is not a problem with outward activity; it is a problem with being. And so it is with humans and sin. Let me explain.

23

It is easy to mistakenly teach children that sin (the breaking of God's law) is merely something that we do, like frogs croak and frogs eats bugs. But croaking or bug-munching is not what makes a frog a frog. It is his very nature, his "personhood," that makes him a frog. And while it is true that sin makes its presence known in the things we do, that is not all sin is. Sin is also our nature, in the same way that a frog is a frog by nature. The breaking or transgressing of God's commandments is what we will always default to apart from the grace of God. If sin were merely what we did outwardly, all we would need in order to please God would be outward, moral reform. Jesus wouldn't have needed to come and be our Savior. But he did come to save us. In fact, he came to give us a new nature because our old nature simply can't be reformed. It needed to be slain and resurrected.

There are many children and adults who are able to stop a certain troubling behavior without becoming a Christian. They may be able to stop because they want some reward more than they want to continue the behavior. For instance, if I tell my son I will pay him $5 a week if he doesn't roll his eyes at me when I ask him to clean his room, that reward might be enough to make him stop his disrespectful behavior. He doesn't need the life, death, and resurrection of Jesus to stop being unkind to me and become pleasing to God. On the other hand, I might be able to motivate him through fear: If I tell him that every time he rolls his eyes at me he will lose his video game privileges, the fear of loss and his love of video games might make him smile compliantly. But what will satisfy me as a parent—desiring outward compliance—is not what will satisfy God, who looks at the heart.

Our problem with sin is actually much deeper than mere outward behavior or any subsequent reform. The Bible tells us that sin is not just what we do. Sin is evident in what we think, and, even worse, it is also evident in why we do what we do (our motives). In fact, sin infects every part of our very nature. So while my son may not be rolling his eyes outwardly, inwardly he may be full of hatred, disrespect, and anger. He may actually be glad that he is able to hide his eye-rolling and take my money. His sin may be multiplied by the fact that he is fooling me while continuing to disrespect me by thinking, *My mom is such an idiot.*

What Is Sin?

One ancient and respected confession of faith defines sin as "any want of or conformity unto, or transgression of, the law of God."[1] Adam and Eve committed the original sin in the garden of Eden when they ate from the Tree of the Knowledge of Good and Evil. When they committed that first sin, when they transgressed or disobeyed God's command, their nature was changed. They became sinners, people incapable of sinlessness. And that sinful nature was passed on to every human being who would ever be born. How did that happen? Adam was our representative, and his choice went for us all. It is as though he was our team captain and he chose heads in the coin toss. Once the coin is flipped, the outcome is sealed. Teammates on the sidelines are not allowed to come out and complain, "Now wait a minute! I didn't choose heads. I don't want heads, I want tails." In just the same way, Adam was our team captain or representative by God's design.

Of course, no matter how much we wish Adam and Eve had not chosen as they did, the truth is that we would have chosen the same way, too. We are born with sin at our very core. It is our nature. It is who we are. We are sinners. And the only hope we have of true transformation—of not simply changing our outward behavior but actually having a new nature—is the death and resurrection of Jesus Christ, with whom we died and rose again. As Paul wrote, "Now if we have died with Christ, we believe that we will also live with him" (Romans 6:8).

What Commands Do We Break?

One day a lawyer came to Jesus and wanted to know what commandment of the Law we need to obey. Jesus answered,

> "You shall love the Lord your God with all your heart and with all your soul and with all your mind and with all your strength." The second is this: "You shall love your neighbor as yourself." There is no other commandment greater than these.
>
> Mark 12:30–31

These commandments tell us we are to love God with everything, absolutely everything we are and have, and to love our neighbors like we love ourselves. But the truth is there has never been a day in your life or mine when we have consistently kept even one of these commands. In fact, our hearts are bent in on ourselves, and we find it impossible to love others every minute of every day of our entire life.

One day I was talking with my son about these very verses and he asked, "What if I snap my fingers? Is snapping a sin?" I asked him if he was snapping his fingers because he loved God and his neighbor. He replied honestly, "No." I said, "Then according to this verse, you have sinned." It is hard to get our minds around that kind of criteria, but Jesus is also the one who said we had to be perfect as our heavenly Father is perfect (Matthew 5:48).

I don't think we take Christ's commands and the life we are called to live seriously enough. We don't understand or feel the full weight of how infected with sin we really are. In part, that's because the world feeds us a steady diet of it's-okay-if-you-are-a-nice-person sprinkled with a bit of if-you-try-your-hardest and topped with a strong drink of you-meant-well.

In teaching us that we must love God and our neighbor 24/7/365, Jesus has obliterated all our "good efforts" and forces us to see that obeying God is something more than being nice. No, as he said, we must "be perfect." And if we aren't perfect, if we fail to love as he has loved, then eternal punishment awaits us.

We are all guilty of watering down God's commands in order to make them more manageable. How can we respond? How can we escape God's just judgment? Our only course of action is to throw ourselves on God's mercy. And that's exactly what we should do. We cannot obey, we sin continually because we are sinners, and we are desperate for a Savior.

I know this all seems pretty harsh. But if we are to have a high view of God's mercy toward sinners, we must have a high view of God's law. Remember the story of the immoral woman in Luke 7? She came into the dinner party and washed Jesus' feet with her tears, drying them with her hair, cleaning them with ointment, and covering them with kisses. Simon, the self-righteous Pharisee, was appalled that Jesus would allow this woman to touch him. He was assured in his heart that he was qualified to sit at the table and eat with Jesus. He was pretty sure he and Jesus were equals, on the same playing field. So Jesus told him a parable:

> "A certain moneylender had two debtors. One owed five hundred denarii, and the other fifty. When they could not pay, he cancelled the debt of both. Now which of them will love him more?" Simon answered, "The one, I suppose, for whom he cancelled the larger debt." And he said to him, "You have judged rightly."
>
> Luke 7:41–43

Simon had a problem: He had made the Law doable. And he thought he was following it. So out of love for Simon, our sweet Savior put the Pharisee's trust in his righteousness to death.

> Do you see this woman? I entered your house; you gave me no water for my feet, but she has wet my feet with her tears and wiped them with her hair. You gave me no kiss, but from the time I came in she has not ceased to kiss my feet. You did not anoint my head with oil, but she has anointed my feet with ointment.
>
> Luke 7:44–46

Jesus held up this immoral woman (probably a prostitute) as an example that Simon needed to follow. I am sure Simon was infuriated by this comparison. But Jesus was not finished with Simon yet. He put a nail in Simon's coffin of morality:

> "Therefore I tell you, her sins, which are many, are forgiven—for she loved much. But he who is forgiven little, loves little." And he said to her, "Your sins are forgiven." Then those who were at table with him began to say among themselves, "Who is this, who even forgives sins?" And he said to the woman, "Your faith has saved you; go in peace."
>
> Luke 7:47–50

Until we parents and our children understand how impossible it is to obey God's laws, we will not love the truth that he has forgiven us. Jesus was teaching Simon that all of the outward obedience, his personal sense of morality, was stopping him from loving God. It was as though he said, *Your good works actually keep you from relationship with me.* Until we see ourselves as being as wicked as a prostitute, we will not cherish God's forgiveness or goodness to us. This is the message we want to give our kids about sin—that sin is more than not sharing a toy with a sibling.

Kids and parents alike should feel desperate about our wretched state. There should be no doubt in our minds that we will never be "good enough." And this knowledge should drive us to the feet of our Savior, which is precisely where the forgiven rest and rejoice.

Sin: The Tasmanian Devil

Do you remember the old Bugs Bunny cartoons? The Tasmanian devil was one of my favorite characters. He would spin around like a tornado, so fast that he was just a blur. When he traveled from place to place, everything around him was destroyed. He would carve up mountainsides, eat everything in his path, and grunt unintelligibly the whole time. His trail of destruction was easy to see. He was a nuisance to everyone around him.

Sin is like the Tasmanian devil. It destroys us and breaks up relationships with God and with our neighbors. It leaves a wide path of destruction. The result of sin in our lives is something that every person will have to face (Romans 3:10–12; Isaiah 53:6). Even when we try to keep it inside of us, in our inward thoughts and motives, it ruins our health. For instance, when we sin by failing to trust God, by worrying all the time, it can affect our blood pressure and our digestion. Like the Tasmanian devil, sin is not to be trifled with. It always ends in death, both spiritually and physically (Romans 6:23). The destruction that follows sin would be our inevitable end, too, were it not for Jesus. He became sin for us so that "we might become the righteousness of God" (2 Corinthians 5:21). This means

> God the Father made Christ to be *regarded and treated* as "sin" even though Christ himself never sinned. . . . Further, we see that God did this *for our sake*—that is, God regarded and treated "our" sin . . . as if our sin belonged to Christ himself.[2]

29

A glorious exchange took place on the cross. All of our sin was placed upon Christ; he took the punishment for all the ways we have failed to obey God's holy law. The second part of the exchange is what he has given us—the righteousness of a life lived in perfect obedience. His obedience was without blemish. It was not just outward obedience, it was also an inward obedience. Every time he obeyed God, he was motivated by a zealous love for his Father. This exchange, this unfathomable exchange, has taken our sin and given us Christ's righteousness.

Why Do We Keep Sinning?

The question that has plagued believers throughout time is: If Christ has paid for all my sin and if I have his perfect record of obedience and if I have a new, transformed nature, *why do I keep sinning, especially when I know it is so wrong?* Although we do not have the mind of God and cannot understand every reason for what he allows, perhaps we can venture a few conjectures.

The apostle Paul dealt with this same problem in his life.

> For I do not understand my own actions. For I do not do what I want, but I do the very thing I hate. Now if I do what I do not want, I agree with the law, that it is good. So now it is no longer I who do it, but sin that dwells within me. For I know that nothing good dwells in me, that is, in my flesh. For I have the desire to do what is right, but not the ability to carry it out. For I do not do the good I want, but the evil I do not want is what I keep on doing. Now if I do what I do not want, it is no longer I who do it, but sin that dwells within me.
>
> Romans 7:15–20

None of us knows why God allows us to continue to struggle with sin like we do, but we can know that part of the reason we sin is so that we can grow in our love for what Christ has done for us by his life, death, and resurrection. Our sin continually strips us of our self-confidence and drives us to hide by the side of the faithful One. Our ongoing sin teaches us how weak we are, which in turn makes us grateful for our weakness and keeps us close to the One who is strong.

Let's be honest: Each one of us has "pet" sins that we allow in our lives. We allow these sins because we enjoy them (sometimes) and because we think we can control them. We don't see that we are slaves to them, but instead foolishly think we are free to do as we choose. We are just like Gollum, the hideous creature in *The Lord of the Rings*. He thought he possessed the Ring of Power but, in fact, the ring (and the power behind it) possessed him. The ring transformed Gollum from Sméagol, a greedy young man, into the creature Gollum, robbing him of his humanity. Sin changes us, too. It destroys us by turning us in on ourselves and robbing our hearts of the ability to love.

The Bad Good News

Our children need to know the terrible reality of sin. If we fail to explain it, they will not see the beauty of God's grace. It is wrong for us to teach them that acting nice outwardly will make Jesus happy. Feigned obedience does not lead to grace. Rather, the Bible teaches us that we needed Jesus to come to earth to live in perfect obedience to all of God's laws. His obedience was outward: He did not steal, murder, or lie, because to do so would violate God's command to love. His obedience was also inward: He loved his Father every moment of every day, and he loved his neighbors (you and me) as himself. In fact, his own testimony about his life was, "I always do the things that are pleasing to him" (John 8:29).

The truth about our sin, our brokenness, and our inability to obey God's overwhelming command to love is meant to crush our self-confidence and force our eyes to look outside of ourselves and our resources to a Redeemer and Rescuer. We need the One who has done it all for us. Sin is terrible; our sin hurts others and ourselves. But, thankfully, it is not up to us to reform ourselves and get rid of our nature. No, the glorious truth is that Jesus has done it for us. He has forgiven us and given us the perfect record of his obedience and full forgiveness.

Once the Holy Spirit moves in our children to show them the ugliness of their sin and the beauty of Christ's love for them, they will begin to long to put away the sin that so easily entangles. Let's not sugarcoat our desperate predicament. Nor should we leave the burden of sin on our children's backs if they have trusted in God to remove it.

Talking to Your Kids

The following may seem repetitive, but it's important to take into account the mental maturity of your children as you talk with them about sin. These truths about sin should make us feel helpless in the face of God's commands. It is good to feel needy in this way. Without recognizing our wretched predicament, we will not be able to lay hold of the great glory of our Savior and his good news, the gospel.

Preschool

Here is a general idea of what you might say to a preschool-aged child about sin and the gospel.

Because God loves us, he has given us rules. When we break his rules, we sin against him. The Bible tells us that sin hurts everyone it touches. Someone's sin is behind most of the tears people shed. Sin and tears go together. The Bible also tells us that when we sin, we deserve punishment. Everyone has to pay for the sins they commit. Jesus promises to pay for your sin. He died to pay for your sin. Everyone needs to be rescued from sin and from the hurt that sin brings. Jesus cried tears, too, but he cried tears when he paid for your sin. Jesus cried those tears because he loves you and knew he had to give his life for you. He was happy to do it because he loves you so much.

We want to be very honest about the destruction and tragedy sin and punishment brings. You can speak often to a preschooler of a Rescuer, too. Let's be careful not to give only the bad news about sin without also giving the good news right along with it.

Ages 5 to 10

At this age kids have had a lot of experience with sin. They have felt the hurt of being sinned against, and they have also intentionally hurt others by sinning against them. They may not have seen the true ugliness and death that sin causes, but they will be familiar with how awful it truly is.

Everyone, including you and me and all our family and friends, are sinners. Every single one of us has disobeyed God's rules. God gives us rules because he loves us and wants us to live happy lives, enjoying him and each other. When we sin, we stop enjoying God. We turn away from his love and we look to other things to make us happy. God has promised there will be punishment for all sin. He tells us that sin always earns death. Most of the time, when you cry tears and feel pain in your heart, it is because of sin. Sin always causes tears. Sin always causes pain. Sin promises that it will make you happy, but it turns on you and hurts you and those around you. The really cool news

33

is that Jesus took all our punishment for all our sin by dying in our place. If you trust in his love and goodness, you can know that God will never punish you for your sin. That's because he has already punished Jesus.

Sin is so much more than what you do, though. Sin is also deep in all of our hearts—it is what we are without God. You see, Jesus cried tears just like we do. But he wasn't crying for his own sin. He was perfect and never sinned. He cried because he took the punishment for your sin so that you could be part of his family. The only thing more powerful than sin is God's love for you and me. God loves to take everything awful and turn it into something beautiful. That is what he can do with your heart.

It is appropriate at this point to start talking with them about how their very nature is to sin against others. The picture we paint must be as bleak as it actually is so the beauty of Christ will shine even brighter. When we talk to children about the universality of sin, we can show them we don't need to be surprised by sin. Sin is just as terrible as the Bible says it is—it touches everyone. This will show your children how desperately the entire world needs a Savior.

Ages 11 and Up

Kids this age will probably have heard about sin from the pulpit, from you, and from their own hearts. They may be so inundated by sin that they have become numb to the realities of sin and its effects on others. It will take the work of the Holy Spirit to convict them of their need for a Savior and open their eyes to the destruction that sin breeds.

You have heard a lot about sin, about what it is and what it does. I am praying that by the grace of God and the work of the Holy Spirit you will see how destructive sin really is.

Sin is so much more than what you do on the outside. It is a deeper problem that isn't solved by learning to be nice. Sin lives within you, and it will create death. In fact, the Bible says your heart is completely dead unless the Holy Spirit makes it alive. Sin creates a terrible mess and never makes anything beautiful. The problem with sin is that it tricks you into thinking it will make you happy, but just the opposite is true. Sin will make you miserable. Although it may feel good in the moment, it will never satisfy you, and it will make you want more.

Sin always brings sadness and tears; it either hurts you or hurts those around you. But God loves to change things up. He is the only One who is more powerful than sin. He actually defeated sin when Jesus died on the cross. Not only did Jesus live a perfect life—never giving in to sin even once, always saying no to every temptation—he also paid the penalty for your sin. He took all the punishment for all your sin when he died on the cross. The punishment you deserve has already been paid—but only if you believe you need rescuing and that Jesus is the Rescuer. Otherwise, you will have to pay for your sins one day. God promises that every sin committed against him will be punished. Either you can be punished for your sin or you can believe that Jesus was punished in your place. The wonderful part is that if you believe Jesus was punished in your place, then right now you are completely clean! I mean completely clean. God doesn't see any remaining sin in your life. All the sins you have committed, all the sins you commit today, and all the sins in your future are already paid for if you believe. Complete forgiveness is yours.

Sin caused the Son of God to cry. The Bible says he cried in the garden of Gethsemane as he thought about paying the penalty for your sin. But he paid that penalty so you would never have to be separated from God. He was separated from his Father so you would always know that God loves you and is with you.

He took the awful ugliness of sin and turned it into the most beautiful relationship.

Parents, you may also want to include a discussion of the two commands: to love God and to love our neighbors. You can tell your children these commands are meant for every second of every day. Many children are wrongly told that if they are nice to others, live nice lives, and make good decisions, then they are good. The obvious problem with this kind of thinking is that it makes them think they don't need a Savior. We have taught them that as long as people (especially Mom and Dad) think they are good, God is happy. The truth is, God is not happy with anything less than perfection. So even if a child tries his hardest, it will not be good enough. He needs something outside of himself to pass the bar of God's judgment; he needs a Savior.

With all of our emphasis on rules and morality, we have denuded the message of the gospel. Martin Luther said, "The law of God, the most [beneficial] doctrine of life, cannot advance man on his way to righteousness, but rather hinders him."[3] Our goal as parents should not be to create a bunch of good kids, but rather to have them see how dead they are and that there is only life in the work of Jesus Christ. So many of our children are like Simon the Pharisee, who sat back and smirked while a prostitute washed Jesus' feet with her tears. We're aghast he would let a sinner touch him. We are taken aback by the inappropriateness of her touch instead of weeping with gratitude for the perfect love of the only One who didn't sin.

May we possess a strong doctrine of sin so that we can hold to the doctrines of grace with passion, just as the woman held the feet of her Savior, weeping, kissing, and rejoicing.

In a Nutshell

- Sin is more than what we do. We sin because it is our nature: We are sinners.
- Sin happens when we break God's law. The first sin occurred in the garden of Eden when Adam and Eve disobeyed God.
- Jesus summarized all of God's law by commanding us to love God and love our neighbor.
- No one has ever achieved this perfection except Jesus Christ. Our sin has caused terrible destruction and suffering in this world.
- We need a Rescuer.
- Christianity is not about being nice; it is the story of how we become "perfectly righteous."
- Even Christians who have had their sins forgiven and have been granted a new nature continue to sin.

3

Why Do People Die?

It's close. You need to come."

I muttered a brief assent, and then set about the task of getting my kids ready to leave. I had been waiting for this day, this call, for months, and yet the news that it might actually happen seemed incomprehensible. I started the car, ready to drive the carload of kids to my friend's home before heading up to the retirement home. My phone rang again, and I hated to answer it because I could guess what I would hear. Reluctantly, I said, "Hello?" It was my mom's voice breaking with sadness. "She's gone."

I hung up and didn't know exactly what I should do. I knew I needed to tell my kids that my grandmother, their great-grandmother, had finally died. I got out of the car and asked my daughter to come with me. She was confused and could see I was crying.

"What, Mommy?" she asked.

"Candy Grandma died," I barely squeaked out.

My sweet baby girl looked at me and began crying with all the heartache I couldn't let myself express. I held her while she cried more.

At that time we were living with my brother and his family. His two children heard her crying and knew what it meant. I breathed the words, "It is good. She is with Jesus now. She isn't suffering anymore." I knew I meant them, but the very words I was using to try to comfort my daughter sounded like dark and meaningless clichés to me.

Eight weeks later I received a similar phone call. This time my mom was calling to say I should come and see my grandfather, as his time to die was drawing near. This time I didn't hesitate. I just got in my car and drove. We got to spend some lovely time with him that evening. He actually responded to my voice, and I could tell he was trying to tell me that he loved me. He seemed to be doing better the next morning, but that evening he joined my grandmother and his Savior in heaven.

As I write this, it has been less than three months since we experienced the awful pain of losing my beautiful grandmother, and less than one month since my gentle grandfather died. There are no words to explain how much they meant to me. I had lived within thirty minutes of them my entire life. Every holiday, every birthday, was spent with them. I would take my kids over to their house every Tuesday to spend time with them. I would purposely go in the afternoon so that my grandmother wouldn't have to make us a meal. But, inevitably, every single Tuesday we would end up having a "second lunch" because she always found a "little something to have a party with."

My heartache is still severe. Since their deaths, there hasn't been a day when I haven't felt the sting of loss. On some days it is excruciating and almost debilitating, while on others it is just a dull ache that lingers in the back of my heart, waiting for an opportunity to push its way forward into my consciousness again.

The book of Ecclesiastes says, "It is better to go to the house of mourning than to go to the house of feasting, for this is the end of all mankind, and the living will lay it to heart" (Ecclesiastes 7:2). Even in the agony of burying my dear grandparents, I can sense that this loss has already brought a change into my heart that I am thankful for. However trite it sounds, I am learning to look at my loved ones in a different way. I am laying to heart the brevity of life. I am grateful for the opportunities to answer the profound questions my children have asked about death during this time. Our conversations have brought an authenticity to our faith.

Death Permeates Our Lives

Children begin to hear about and see images of death at a very young age. It is a universal part of our human experience, but our culture also portrays images of death on television and in video games while the rest of the world sees death all around them on a daily basis.

Death is everywhere, part of the warp and woof of life in a sin-cursed world, so we should not try to shield our children from knowing about it, nor should we try to avoid talking about it. We really can't shelter our children from the knowledge of death, no matter how we might want to. All our children need do is walk outside and see a dead bug, watch a leaf fall from a tree, or see a patch of dead grass to know that death is, in fact, the one constant in all of life.

Like you, I want my children to grow up in a world where there is no pain or sadness, where there is nothing to fear. But out of love for my children, I have to resist the temptation to portray the world as a utopian paradise. Telling them the truth is actually a kindness to them, because in doing so we are preparing them to understand and face the reality of both life and death. While they are in our care, we have the opportunity to help them begin to think through the most difficult topics.

Please don't misunderstand: I am not saying we should expose our kids to every form of entertainment, nor am I saying that the way the media portrays death is beneficial or good. Video games, television, movies, and even some children's novels glamorize death and desensitize us to the deep pain it produces. Wise parents should discern the difference between a beneficial discussion about the realities of death and the foolish portrayal of death in our culture.

Help your children know that they can talk to you about death—don't avoid it or over-dramatize it. Children need to know that sin has had a serious and devastating effect on the world, and we should not fear that addressing death in realistic terms will create an unhealthy preoccupation, superstition, or fear within them. Again, when we fail to teach our children the realities of life and death, sin, and the suffering it has occasioned, they will search for the answers outside of the home or within themselves.

What Are They Mature Enough to Hear?

Even though we want to engage children in this serious topic, we need to be aware of their individuality and ability to understand. Speak to them in a way that will bring truth and comfort at a level they can grasp. What follows is a general guideline of what you might expect from children in differing age groups. I will caution that these are not hard and fast rules. Different children have different needs and develop in different stages. You should know your children by asking them questions and listening to their answers.

> Studies show that children go through a series of stages in their understanding of death. For example, preschool children usually see death as reversible, temporary, and impersonal. Watching cartoon characters on television miraculously recover after being crushed or blown apart tends to reinforce this idea.
>
> Between the ages of 5 and 9, most children are beginning to realize that death is final and that all living things die. But they still do not see death as personal. They harbor the idea that somehow they can escape through their own ingenuity. During this stage, children also tend to personify death. They may associate death with a skeleton or with the angel of death. Some children have nightmares about these images.
>
> From age 9 or 10 through adolescence, children begin to comprehend fully that death is irreversible; that all living things die and that they, too, will die someday. Some begin to work on developing philosophical views of life and death. Teenagers often become intrigued with seeking the meaning of life. Some adolescents react to their fear of death by taking unnecessary chances with their lives.[1]

Our children need to know that the Christian faith does not portray an unrealistic world where everything is perfect, nor does it avoid addressing the painful, hard-to-understand things of life. Christianity is for real people with real problems.

Out of all the world's religions, ours is the only one that deals with death in a hope-giving yet realistic way. We recognize the inevitability of death for all, but we also recognize that even though we may precede Christ's second advent in our death, he has promised to "bring with him those who have fallen asleep" (1 Thessalonians 4:14). Even the finality of death is revoked in the reappearing of the living One. Our death is not the end of our life, only our physical life here.

Jesus Christ understands by experience both death and life. Because of this, we are the only faith community that has a God who understands grief and loss. Jesus, the Son of God, was actually described as "a man of sorrows, and acquainted with grief" (Isaiah 53:3).

As we have drifted from the gospel message of a suffering Servant who tasted death "for everyone" (Hebrews 2:9), we have embraced a hopeless message more like "be good, and good things will happen." This is not the Christianity that Jesus taught. He is our suffering Savior. God the Father knows the grief of losing a son. Jesus himself wept at Lazarus's tomb when he faced the death of his friend. Jesus knew that he had the power to raise Lazarus from the dead, and yet he cried because his friend had died. He grieved over the effects of sin and the way that death rips lives apart. He knew a heaviness of heart as he walked with his dear friends Martha and Mary. He experienced their pain. He was fully a man and felt the pain of death and the destruction it caused a beloved family.

This understanding of Christianity can bring comfort to children; they can know that Christ also had to face the anguish of losing a friend. Experiencing grief and sadness at death is not sinful, but avoiding teaching our children about the realities of our faith, life, and death is. It is wrong not only because they are missing out on the peace and freedom that comes from knowing that God is in control of everything (even death), but also because they will be left with their own ideas and confusion. When we fail to speak to children about death, they will have to interpret events in their own way. Here's a story from a child psychologist that helps illustrate this:

Mark, who was then five years old, had been brought in by his parents who were concerned about his refusal to go to bed at night. Although he had no history of bedtime problems previously, Mark had begun to throw bedtime tantrums two weeks earlier. He would cry and refuse to go near the bedroom, and, when finally overcome with sleep, he would often awaken with nightmares. . . .

During one of the play sessions I had with Mark, he told me the story of a man who "got a heart attack, fell out of bed, and died." He explained that he had overheard his mother telling this story to someone over the telephone. Putting events together with the help of his parents, I learned that a family friend had recently died of a heart attack, and Mark did indeed hear his mother describe the event to a friend over the telephone. Mark had no idea what a heart attack was or where one came from. He certainly knew what falling out of bed was, though, and if doing that could make you get a heart attack and die, then no one was going to get him into a bed.

With this information I was able to help ease Mark's concerns in short order, but the concreteness of his concerns remains an impressive example of the misconceptions children can develop about death.[2]

As you can see, having open and honest dialogue with kids, not trying to hide the truth from them, may be a great benefit.

Talk About It Before You Need To

It is important to have built a firm foundation with your kids about the death of a loved one even before they have to experience it personally. You shouldn't wait until a dear family member or friend dies to bring the topic up. If you wait, you will be grappling with your own faith and emotions. Trying to talk to your children about death then will be unnecessarily difficult.

During the time of loss, your heart and mind will be reeling, and you will not want to build the basic blocks of theology with your kids.

In those trying times, you will find that the more you have already shared, the better equipped you will all be to deal with your loss and theirs. The more you talk about it outside of crisis, the better understanding you will all have during crisis. Death will inevitably affect your life, and when it does, you will find that all you have taught them will be incredibly beneficial.

Talking With Your Kids

I want to mention again that each child is different. Just because they fall into a certain age range does not mean they can developmentally handle certain truths, or that they can't handle more than what I am going to suggest here. Please make the effort to know your child first. I wouldn't suggest reading the following explanations directly to your child. Instead, you might begin a conversation and then watch to see if they are interested. Interacting with them personally is always better than reading a script. Below is a framework for ideas that you could incorporate into a conversation about death.

Preschool

When God first created the world, there was no death. But when Adam and Eve sinned, they brought death into the world. Sin is disobeying God. Sin hurts everything it touches. It is kind of like an ugly weed that comes into a beautiful garden and makes it a big mess. When Adam and Even sinned, they broke what was beautiful and perfect, but that is not the end of the story. Everyone will die someday, but we don't have to be afraid of death. Jesus came to the world and made a way so that we can have life forever. Jesus even said that he has won the fight with death. We know this because when he died, he was stronger than death, and he came back to life again. We will die here on earth, but if you are one of God's kids, you will come back to life, too. Then you will live forever with him in his house. You will be in the best place. Everything that was once broken will be fixed, and it will never break again. In our forever home, heaven, there will be no more death, no more sadness, no more tears.

Again, this is only a general idea of what you could say. The important parts to make sure you express are that death was not the original plan, death is a result of sin, Jesus defeated death so we don't need to fear, and heaven awaits those who are God's children.

Ages 5 to 10

This is a trickier age to talk to about death, so we are incorporating everything that might be said to any child over the age of five according to their maturity level and what they have experienced. In fact, it might be one of the most difficult ages because nightmares abound at this age, and the words you use need to be chosen carefully. They understand that death is final but yet don't seem to have the mental maturity to deal with that thought.

You know that when God first created everything there was no death in the world. We would have lived forever with each other and with him. But when Adam and Eve sinned, death entered the world. Anytime sin shows up, life always gets messed up. Sin occurs when we don't obey God—when we choose what we want over what he wants. Each of us will die, but we don't have to be afraid of death if we are Christians. I know that death seems scary because it is forever, but there is something stronger than death. The One who created life can also destroy death. Do you know who that is? The Bible tells us that Jesus created all things, and all things were created for him and through him. Jesus is the One who has beaten death. He died so that he could pay for our sins, but he also rose from the dead. He came back to life, and because he conquered death, his promise is that all who love him will, too. The promise is that you will come back to life like he did and will live with him forever in heaven. Heaven is the one place where death will never be able to hurt anybody again. We will live forever with him there. In our forever home there will be nothing sad, nothing that makes us sick, nothing that makes us cry; there will only be happiness and love forever.

This might be a good time, depending on the age and maturity of your children, to also begin talking to them about the realities of hell.

I want you to understand there isn't just a heaven for God's children and then nothing else for the rest of the people. There is a place called hell, and that place was made for the devil and all the people who do not believe they need God. The Bible promises there will be punishment for all sin. You have been given two options: The first is that you can believe you are a sinner and you need someone to take that punishment for you. If you believe Jesus died on the cross for your sins, then he promises he has already taken all the punishment for all of your sin. The other option is that you have to pay for your sin. The punishment for sin is so great that if we choose to pay for it ourselves, it will take all of eternity. We can never pay for the way we have sinned against God; there is not enough time. In hell, everyone who didn't believe in God will experience the anger of God against sin forever. But Jesus has already experienced the anger of God against sin for those who believe—for Christians. If you believe in him, then he took your punishment, and God has no anger left for you. Hell is only for those who do not want to be with God and his Son, Jesus Christ.

This is a chilling, sobering message, isn't it? Let us use wisdom and pray for guidance of the Holy Spirit to know how much to say and when to say it. We don't want to use the fear of hell or punishment as a motivation for conversion. Fear may frighten children for a little while, but love will transform them for a lifetime. If you are going to have this conversation, it might also be good to talk to children about how Jesus' heart breaks for those who will know eternal pain. He wept when he looked out over Jerusalem and was saddened by the people's hardness of heart. God does not send people to hell with sadistic glee. He does it with a commitment to his character that should make us treasure the mercy we have received.

Ages 11 and Up

This is a wide age range and will take a lot of prayer and wisdom on your part to know where your kid falls in his understanding. These are the ages where you can really start opening up the realities of all of death to your kids. Feel free to draw on everything I have recommended to be said to younger children, but you can do so now in more biblical terms. Make sure you are asking your children questions to ascertain whether they understand what you are saying or not. Have your children explain to you what they think you are saying, making sure you define terms they misunderstand.

Children this age definitely need to know about the truth of heaven and hell. They need to know everyone will die and that Jesus Christ has conquered death. Not only did Jesus conquer death by dying on the cross and then rising from the dead, but he also took the most powerful force on earth and bent it to his will. He used death to complete his plan of redemption. Death's work is to destroy; Jesus used death to open the door to life. This ultimate paradox can give hope in even the most hopeless of situations. This knowledge fights any fear of death. As they are able, you can also get into more nuanced conversations with your young people.

Is Death a Punishment?

Death is not a punishment to believers. If someone gets sick and he is a Christian, it does not mean God is angry with him. Death is a result of our sinful nature, but it is not a punishment for believers, because Jesus Christ has already taken all the punishment, all of the wrath for your sin and for mine. He was our propitiation, our wrath-bearer. He did not bear the wrath and punishment that was due us only halfway. He is either our sacrificial Lamb or he isn't. If we tell kids that Aunt Fran got cancer because her faith wasn't strong enough or because she did something wrong, we are teaching them a false, anti-gospel theology. We are not conveying the lesson Jesus taught his disciples in John 9:

> And his disciples asked him, "Rabbi, who sinned, this man or his parents, that he was born blind?" Jesus answered, "It was not that this man sinned, or his parents, but that the works of God might be displayed in him. We must work the works of him who sent me while it is day; night is coming, when no one can work. As long as I am in the world, I am the light of the world."
>
> vv. 2–5

God does not choose to heal some and let others die based on the quality of their faith. He chooses to heal some and let others die based on what glorifies him most; we see that in the story of Lazarus mentioned earlier. Jesus said the reason he delayed coming—the reason Lazarus died—was to help those around him to believe, to believe he held the power of life and death. Jesus allowed Lazarus to die to glorify God. It was important for those around Jesus to see that he did have the power to raise others from the dead for two reasons: first, to show them he could have stopped his own crucifixion if he so desired, and second, to give them hope after his death that death wasn't the final word.

If any healing from sin or disease rested on the quality of a sinner's faith, there would be no healing ever. That's because the requirement is perfection, and the only human who ever had perfect faith was Jesus, the same One who took all the punishment for our sins. He took our sins and bore our judgment away.

Suicide

Young people in this age range will become aware of suicide. They need to have a basic understanding of what the Bible says about suicide. The Bible does not teach that suicide is an unforgiveable sin. Committing suicide is a sin because it is a murder of oneself, but again, nowhere do we read that a true believer won't be forgiven of all his sin, confessed or not.

Suicide does cause unimaginable pain for the ones who are left behind. We can trust, though, that Christ will see all those affected by a loved one's suicide through their immense pain. Jesus knows the pain of loss, and he has promised to sympathize with the suffering (Hebrews 4:15). He bears their grief upon his heart. We can also explain to our children that each one of us makes selfish decisions that hurt others every single day, and yet we are forgiven. This will hopefully soften our hearts and sap the anger against the deceased.

Conclusion

Death is a certainty, but Christ's love is a much stronger reality. Although death is our enemy and is against all that is good, we can know it will be the last enemy to be defeated. In one sense it already has been defeated, and yet it still has a certain power. On the last day, death will be defeated completely. We read about this glorious truth in 1 Corinthians 15:

> Now if Christ is proclaimed as raised from the dead, how can some of you say that there is no resurrection of the dead? But if there is no resurrection of the dead, then not even Christ has been raised. And if Christ has not been raised, then our preaching is in vain and your faith is in vain. We are even found to be misrepresenting God, because we testified about God that he raised Christ, whom he did not raise if it is true that the dead are not raised. For if the dead are not raised, not even Christ has been raised. And if Christ has not been raised, your faith is futile and you are still in your sins. Then those also who have fallen asleep in Christ have perished. If in Christ we have hope in this life only, we are of all people most to be pitied.
>
> But in fact Christ has been raised from the dead, the firstfruits of those who have fallen asleep. For as by a man came death, by a man has come also the resurrection of the dead. For as in Adam all die, so also in Christ shall all be made alive. But each in his own order: Christ the firstfruits, then at his coming those who belong to Christ. Then comes the end, when he delivers the kingdom to God the Father after destroying every rule and every authority and power. For he must reign until he has put all his enemies under his feet. The last enemy to be destroyed is death. For "God has put all things in subjection under his feet." But when it says, "all things are put in subjection," it is plain that he is excepted who put all things in subjection under him. When all things are subjected to him, then the Son himself will

also be subjected to him who put all things in subjection under him, that God may be all in all.

vv. 12–28

The truth of Christ's resurrection from the dead gives us ultimate and final hope that we, too, shall be raised, and we will reign forever with him. As sad as death is, resurrection will be all the more glorious. We have hope, we have answers, and we can share the beauty and power of our faith with our children. We are not consigned to suffer and live hard lives and then die without hope. Our existence is so much more. There is a Savior who knows the pain of loved ones dying, who has experienced the darkness of death, and yet who now has the victory over all. This is the Savior we can and must share with our children.

In a Nutshell

- Death comes to everyone and every living thing.
- Death is caused by sin, but not necessarily by specific sins.
- Although a Christian may die, Christ promised that a Christian will be resurrected just like he was to live with him forever.
- For the Christian, death is not a punishment; it is a release from this sin-cursed world to be with Jesus.

4

Who Is Satan? What Is Hell?

As much as we wish it were otherwise, our children probably hear more about Satan and demons from the media than they hear about Jesus, the Rescuer. Most children have seen cartoons or commercials wrongly depicting Satan as a spookily horned creature with a red face and a pitchfork tail. And as inaccurate as that portraiture is, Satan is pleased when we spend any time thinking about him—and he's especially smug if we or our children either live in fear of him or think a personal evil that is at work in the world to "steal and kill and destroy" (John 10:10) doesn't exist.

Of course, this chapter will not be a complete study on the topic of Satan, his role in the world, and his enlistment of demons and people in his wicked schemes. There is so much more to say than we will have room for, and also so much that is unknown. The Bible does not answer every question we might have; it does promise, however, to answer everything we need to know so that we can live profitable lives for God's glory (2 Timothy

3:16–17). If you find your children have more questions than this brief chapter answers, please consider the recommended resources at the back of this book.

First Things First

As we delve into these murky waters, let us begin by remembering who God is. What he has said about himself, who he is, and what his purposes are will be the foundation not only of this chapter but of every chapter in this book. God has declared that he is supremely wise (Romans 16:27), supremely powerful (1 Chronicles 29:11), and supremely loving (1 John 4:8). So as we consider this topic as well as all the topics in this book, this will be our starting place—our foundation and our ending point. Understanding God's character will light our way safely over the floods of confusion and through the dungeons of doubt.

The Prince of Darkness Grim

Pastor and author Sam Storms described Satan in this way:

> The first thing to remember about Satan is that he, like all other angels, was created at a point in time (John 1:1–3; Colossians 1:16). Satan is not eternal. He is a finite creature. He is, therefore, *God's* Devil. Satan is *not* the equal and opposite power of God (contra *dualism*). His power is not infinite. He does not possess divine attributes. In sum, he is no match for God! At most, Satan is the equal and opposite power of the archangel Michael.[1]

Let me explain the term *dualism* in a way that may be a bit more understandable when you're thinking of talking with your children about it. In the epic sci-fi film trilogy STAR WARS (I refuse to include the prequels; I am a purist), the dark side and the force were the two opposing forces. They had equal power, and it was up to humans to decide which side they would give themselves to, and which force they would use. As the story goes, whichever force had the stronger human became the more powerful of the two.

STAR WARS is a perfect example of dualism, and as entertaining as those movies might be, they are completely unbiblical. God and Satan are not two equal and opposing forces, because God is supreme and the creator of all there is, including Satan. God always wins. His power is always supreme. In fact, God rules over Satan in such a way that Satan has to ask permission from God anytime he desires to attack one of God's children (see Job 1:12; 2:6; 1 Corinthians 10:13; Revelation 20:2, 7).

Jesus Crushed Satan

In the garden of Eden, after Satan first wrought his terrible work by tempting Eve and Adam to distrust God, the Lord promised that one of Eve's descendants (Mary's Son, Jesus) would crush the serpent's head (Genesis 3:14). He did just that, as New Testament writers testify:

> Since therefore the children share in flesh and blood, he himself likewise partook of the same things, that through death he might destroy the one who has the power of death, that is, the devil.
>
> Hebrews 2:14

> The reason the Son of God appeared was to destroy the works of the devil.
>
> 1 John 3:8

He [God] disarmed the rulers and authorities and put them to open shame, by triumphing over them in him [Jesus].

Colossians 2:15

And the great dragon was thrown down, that ancient serpent, who is called the devil and Satan, the deceiver of the whole world—he was thrown down to the earth, and his angels were thrown down with him.

Revelation 12:9

While dying on the cross for our sins, Jesus was also destroying the work and power of Satan. We can be assured that Jesus accomplished this feat because he cried out "It is finished" from the cross (John 19:30). Jesus knew his act of obedience and sacrifice would forever unmake all the evil Satan had sewn into the world. We know for certain that Satan's doom is sealed.

We Share in His Victory

Because of our union with Jesus, Christians are also told that Satan must flee from us if we resist his temptations (1 Peter 5:9; James 4:7; Ephesians 4:27; 6:11, 13). Although Satan does still have some power in the world, his power is limited. It is weak compared to the power of the risen Savior. Christ defeated him, stripped from him every tool in his arsenal, and as we resist him in the strength Christ supplies, he cannot have his way with us, either. Yes, Satan does prowl "around like a roaring lion, seeking someone to devour," but all he can do is roar at us and try to frighten us. We can "resist him" by standing "firm in [our] faith" (1 Peter 5:8–9) in what Jesus has already done for us. This is incredibly encouraging, for we know that victory does not lie in our own strength of resisting, but in Christ, the "Lion of the tribe of Judah" (Revelation 5:5). He has already conquered! Remember that Satan tried unsuccessfully to tempt Jesus to disobey as Adam had, but Jesus chose instead to do his Father's will at every turn, and in that obedience Satan's ability to condemn us was destroyed.

Satan's temptations in the life of the believer are threefold: He accuses us, flatters us, and besmirches God's goodness.

First, Satan is the accuser, which is what his name means (Luke 4:2, 13; Revelation 12:9, 12). He accuses us of being too sinful—of having gone too far from God to ever be welcomed back to him. Satan's accusations fly right at the heart of the gospel. While it is true we are sinners, our sin does not stop God from loving us. In line with what pastor and writer Tim Keller has expressed, you are more sinful and flawed than you ever dared believe, and also more loved and welcomed than you ever dared hope.[2] Satan reminds us of our sin and insinuates that we have crossed over into an area where God's grace cannot reach. He never tires of reminding us of our sin. But the Bible says God has removed those sins from us, "as far as the east is from the west" (Psalm 103:12). Satan lies to us and says there are sins we can commit that God will not forgive. Satan's desired result in accusing us in this way is to entice us to despair and hide away from God (Genesis 3:8). Satan tempts us to forget or doubt the love and forgiveness that is promised to us, if we would look to Christ and live.

Satan also accuses us of being good and not needing God. Now, this might be a little confusing. Let me explain. Satan brings our "righteousness" up before our eyes continually. He reminds us of how good we have been over and over again. We start to forget the first part of the gospel, that we are more sinful and flawed than we ever dared believe. We can't and, quite frankly, wouldn't want to relate to Paul, when he calls himself the "chief of sinners." Satan's desired result is that again we will hide from God, our only source of hope, and begin to hope in ourselves. We think we don't need him. Our reasoning is as follows: *If I am not that bad, why would I need a Savior?* We might not ever voice those words, but this belief is the underlying problem when we experience a weak prayer life, self-righteous anger at others' sin, lack of joy, and lack of compassion.

Satan also accuses God of not being worthy of our undying affection. In the book of Job and in Jesus' temptation in the wilderness, we observe this happening. He blasphemes the Lord, saying the only reason people worship him is because of the good gifts he gives.

Our Enemy's Tactics

Satan's goal is to attack God's children and make us question God's goodness. You can clearly see this demonstrated in the book of Job. Satan physically attacked Job, but never without the permission of the all-powerful One. The Enemy takes great delight in bringing physical and mental destruction upon people. And he uses people, especially unbelievers, to accomplish his goals. Sam Storms writes:

> Paul says Satan is "at work" in the "sons of disobedience" (Mark 3:17; Luke 10:6; 16:8; 20:34; Acts 4:26; Ephesians 5:8; 1 Peter 1:14), a phrase used earlier of God's activity in the world (Ephesians 1:11) in general in the resurrection of Jesus in particular (1:20). Here it refers to Satan's supernatural activity by which he exerts a negative influence over the lives of unbelievers. This does *not* mean that all unbelievers are demon-possessed. It does mean that the whole world lies *in the power of* the evil one.[3]

Satan's work is always to hurt and destroy. The beauty of our God is that he takes Satan's work and turns it on its head. He takes all the awful things Satan does in the believer's life and "works [them] together for our good" (Romans 8:28).

Satan is also called the "tempter" (Matthew 4:3), which is exactly how we are introduced to him in Genesis 3 when he enters the story of creation. Here he tempts Adam and Eve by accusing God. He convinces them God is selfish and unloving. His words breed unbelief in them. At Satan's word they disobey the law of God and eat the forbidden fruit. Not surprisingly, he tries the same tactic when tempting Christ in Matthew 4:1–11. But where Adam and Eve failed, Christ triumphed. He proved that Satan's lies and temptations were not invincible and that by the power of the Holy Spirit, Satan can be resisted. Jesus resisted the devil's schemes and fought back with God's own words.

His Doom Is Sure

Lastly, we know Satan's ultimate demise is sure. Revelation 20:10 says,

> And the devil who had deceived them was thrown into the lake of fire and sulfur where the beast and the false prophet were, and they will be tormented day and night forever and ever.

Although we do endure Satan's accusations, attacks, and temptations during our earthly lives, there will come a day when all that conflict will end. The doom that is already sealed will come to pass. Until that day, we pray for strength to resist; believe in God's control, love, and wisdom; and praise the Son for his work in conquering the devil.

What About Demons?

Demons, like the devil, are created beings. They are angels who have chosen to pledge their alliance to the prince of darkness. Their work is the same as that of their master, to destroy the work of the gospel. Sam Storms points to 1 Corinthians 10:14–22 when he explains, "Demons animate and energize all non-Christian religions and all forms of idolatry."[4]

Demons can indwell humans or other created beings in order to complete their work (Mark 5:3; Acts 19:16; Luke 9:39). They are powerful, intelligent, and evil. Again, just like their leader, their doom is sure. It is sure because of Christ's completed work, his life, death, resurrection, and reign. Paul teaches us that God "disarmed the rulers and authorities and put them to open shame, by triumphing over them in [Christ]" (Colossians 2:15).

On the cross, Christ defeated the power of demons. Christians have been given that same power: "Behold, I have given you authority to tread on serpents and scorpions, and over all the power of the enemy, and nothing shall hurt you" (Luke 10:19). While this is exciting news and we can take great comfort in it, here is verse 20: "Nevertheless, do not rejoice in this, that the spirits are subject to you, but rejoice that your names are written in heaven." Satan and demons love to get our eyes off of the glorious truths in verse 20. They love to get us thinking about them, fearing them, or conversely sensationalizing them, making them the primary focus of our faith. Jesus speaks directly to any propensity we might have to focus on demons and says, "Keep your eyes on me and my work." There is nothing Satan and his demons hate more than to play second fiddle to the Son of God.

Although the topic of demons creates much confusion, we can learn from their interactions with Christ. They feared Christ and begged him not to torment them (Mark 5:7; Luke 8:31). They had to obey him. When Jesus told them to leave people alone, they did. They also knew Jesus was the Son of God (Mark 1:23–27; 9:25–26; Acts 16:18). They even testify to the work of Christ (Acts 16:16–17). We must note that even though they obey, fear, and believe Christ is the Son of God and know that he brought salvation, they are against Christ. The only thing that makes you a true follower of Christ is that you have trusted him and transferred your trust from your own work to the work of another. Demons hate Christ for his goodness and kindness and because he loves the Father, whom they hate.

Satan and his army are not only against God and his army, they are also against unbelievers. They torment and hurt even those who hate God. They use and abuse those who are on their team. But God, who is rich in mercy, has come to turn all of that around. He frees those who have been tormented—those under the rule of Satan—and gives them back their right minds. He frees them physically, spiritually, and mentally from the bonds of the evil one.

Judgment and Hell

The end for Satan and his followers is sure. It is promised as a form of judgment to all who do not accept God's free gift of grace in Christ. Hell is mentioned over fifty times in the Bible; it is not a side note. It is a real place where real people go and where the devil and his demons will spend all of eternity. Hebrews 9:27 says, "It is appointed for man to die once, and after that comes judgment." There is a place of judgment and anguish that we cannot even begin to comprehend. Just as we cannot comprehend the beauty, brilliance, and joy of heaven, so we cannot comprehend the torture, pain, and anguish of hell.

The Bible describes hell as a place of "outer darkness," where there will be "weeping and gnashing of teeth" (Matthew 25:30). It is a place where there is "eternal and unquenchable fire and punishment" (Matthew 25:41, 46; Mark 9:43), where "the worm does not die" (Mark 9:48). This description is again telling us of unstoppable, unending torment. One of the more terrifying descriptions of hell appears in Revelation 14:10–11:

> He also will drink the wine of God's wrath, poured full strength into the cup of his anger, and he will be tormented with fire and sulfur in the presence of the holy angels and in the presence of the Lamb. And the smoke of their torment goes up forever and ever, and they have no rest, day or night.

This cup of God's wrath was what Christ begged would be taken from him on the night before his crucifixion. Luke 22:42–44 reads:

> "Father, if you are willing, remove this cup from me. Nevertheless, not my will, but yours, be done." And there appeared to him an angel from heaven, strengthening him. And being in an agony he prayed more earnestly; and his sweat became like great drops of blood falling down to the ground.

This cup of God's wrath is promised to everyone who sins (Romans 6:23). Everyone will either drink it for all of eternity or they will trust that Christ drank it for them. How awful must that cup be if the God-man could not bear the thought of drinking it!

As we have covered these confusing and terrifying subjects, we must see the hope that even this discussion brings to us. We must not lose sight that Christ has conquered death, he has defeated Satan, he has given us authority and power over demons, and he has consumed the dreadful cup of God's wrath for our sin. Although we must never lose sight of the sobering warnings about hell and the work of the devil and his demons, we can rest in the knowledge of the power of our God.

Talking to Your Kids

So now the hard part: How do we talk to our kids about this without giving them nightmares? Again, let me start by saying, know your children. Some children may be able to understand and hear more without it being a constant source of terror in their lives. Other children may just need the basics and then lots of encouragement about the power of God. The topics we have covered in this chapter are difficult to understand. It is appropriate and helpful to let your children know you feel that way, too. When children have doubts, worries, or fears, it is okay to let them know you feel the same way. We don't have to pretend to be "super-Christians" for them. We can tell them that even though we don't completely understand all of the horrors of hell, the devil, demons, and the final judgment, we can trust that God's ways are higher than our ways, and his thoughts are higher than our thoughts. We can go back to our starting place—praying for faith to believe and trust in the character of God. The truth of the Bible doesn't depend on whether humans understand all of it. It would actually be a travesty to have a God who thinks and reasons like a human.

Preschool

Please interact with your children, hear their concerns. You don't need to over-explain these topics with preschool-age kids. You should be aware that they will see images of the devil in cartoons, where the "bad" person typically goes to a place with fire when he dies, and the "good" person ends up floating on the clouds, strumming a harp, wearing white. Cartoons tend to make hell less terrifying than it is, but they also make heaven less exciting than it is.

Satan was created by God. He is not as powerful as God is. Just like if you make a Lego ship or color a picture, you created it, and you can smash your Legos or tear the picture up. God is in control of Satan. Satan likes to hurt, but God loves to help. Jesus came to earth to beat Satan. The Bible says God did just that. The Bible also tells us that everyone must pay for sin. Either you will pay for your sin in hell, which is a very sad and terrible place, or you can believe that Jesus came to pay for all your sin. He did that when he died on the cross. Even though hell and the devil are not nice things to think about, we can always remember that God is the most powerful, most loving, and the smartest. He will always win. He has already won. So if we are Christians, we don't need to be afraid.

As you might have noticed, I didn't mention demons in the previous paragraph. I think kids this age are usually too young for this information.

Ages 5 to 10

The devil was created. He was an angel who decided at one point he didn't want to follow or obey God. He then became the ruler of all the evil in the world. Even though he is the ruler of evil, he is not as powerful as God. Matter of fact, it isn't even close. When Jesus came to earth, he conquered Satan. Satan has already lost the war, but he goes on fighting for now. One day, when Jesus comes back, he will make all the sadness come untrue. On that day he will send Satan to hell forever. Hell is the saddest, most terrible place you can think of. Everyone who doesn't trust Christ to be his or her Savior will spend eternity in hell with Satan and his demons. Demons were once angels, also, but they chose to follow Satan. Satan and his demons go around trying to hurt and bring sadness. It may be a little confusing why God would let them continue their terrible work.

We must believe that God knows better than we do. It would seem so simple just to destroy Satan and his demons and have that be the end of it. But God is much wiser than we are, and he has decided for right now that the thing that will make more people love him is to let Satan live. You can know for a fact that God is stronger than Satan. Satan has to ask for permission before he does anything to one of God's kids. Nothing in all of creation (including the devil and his workers) is out of God's control. So even though these thoughts might be a little scary and hard to understand, we can hold on to the truth that God is bigger, stronger, and smarter than the devil. God loves us and will always be with us.

If your child is not mature enough to handle all these truths, just use what I suggested for preschoolers. The point is not to scare or to dumb down, but to pray that they understand the gravity of these topics while also remembering who is really in charge.

Ages 11 and Up

Satan is the most evil being ever created. It is important to re-member that he was created, because that means the Creator is more powerful. Satan wasn't always evil. God would not create anything evil. At one point he was a good angel who decided he didn't want to obey God. Satan wants to bring hate and sadness and pain to everyone he touches. His name means "accuser." He wants to go around reminding everyone of their sins so they lose hope that their Savior will love and welcome them. He wants to tempt you, to make you believe something else is more important or will bring more happiness than God. Satan wants to attack you. He hates God and God's kids. He also hates those who don't belong to God. He's so evil he even attacks his own followers. His main goal is to bring destruction and hatred into the world.

67

Demons work for Satan. You see, Satan doesn't have the same power as God, so he can't be everywhere at once. He uses demons to do his work. Satan is also not as wise as God. The Bible said he "entered Judas" in order to use him to kill Jesus. Satan didn't even realize he was helping God. Satan thought killing Jesus would win the battle. The truth was, Jesus laid down his life willingly, and that was what won the battle. Jesus came to destroy the power of the devil. He did just that when he gave us full forgiveness of sins. Every time you feel accused of a past sin, you can remember that Jesus died to forgive that very sin. Remembering you are forgiven because of what Jesus has done is what defeats Satan. One day, there will be a final judgment for all created beings. On that day everyone will have to give an account—an explanation—for their lives. Those who have loved God and trusted Christ to be their goodness will be with God in heaven forever. Those who have decided that God wasn't who they wanted to follow and obey will end up spending eternity with Satan and his demons in hell.

Hell is described as a place of unimaginable pain and suffering. Those in hell will sin against God in anger every day for eternity, and every day for eternity they will be punished for sin. This may seem a bit extreme and harsh, but sinning against God and refusing his gift is just that terrible. God's judgment is just. While these topics are a bit unsettling and confusing to us, we are not to focus on the power of Satan or his demons. God could destroy them at any minute, and although that may seem like a good idea to us, we have to remember that God is smarter than we can even imagine. We have to trust he knows what is best. We have to trust he loves us the most. We have to trust he is good and would never do anything contrary to his goodness.

You may want to incorporate other truths discussed earlier in the chapter. We want to build confidence in God's power and his goodness, not fear. We also want our children to see that hell is not some eternal party where all the bad people go to have fun.

As we share these truths with our children, we must remember that our words, although important, will not make or break their belief in God. He is the author of salvation, and bringing our kids to him is his work to complete.

In a Nutshell

- God created the angel who became Satan.
- Satan is not as powerful as God but is part of his creation.
- We don't know why God allows Satan to live, but we do know a day will come when God will throw Satan and all his demons into hell.
- Jesus came to destroy the works of the devil and was victorious over him.
- God will punish all sin. He will either punish it by abandoning unbelievers to hell, or he has already punished it by pouring out his wrath on his Son. Believers can know that God no longer has any wrath left for them.

5

Why Do People Get Divorced?

Because this book was written with the Christian faith community in view, you might wonder why we're including a chapter on divorce. Or perhaps you're not wondering at all because you've seen the prevalence and devastation in your own life or in the lives of others in your church. It's axiomatic to say that divorce is a part of everyone's day-to-day life—yes, even in the church.

Here are some sobering statistics:

- In America, there will be one divorce every thirteen seconds. That's 6,646 divorces per day and 46,523 divorces per week.[1] What this means is that in the time it took for you to read that sentence, one family was breaking apart. It also means that from the time you got up this morning until you lie down tonight, over 6,500 marriages will end.

- Forty-three percent of children growing up in America today are being raised without their fathers.[2] The far-reaching consequences of the absentee father are beyond description.

- Half of all American children will witness the breakup of a parent's marriage. Of these children, close to half will also see the breakup of a parent's second marriage.[3]

- Forty-one percent of first marriages will end in divorce. Sixty percent of second marriages will end in divorce. Seventy-three percent of third marriages will end in divorce.[4]

- Around 1 million children are affected by divorce each year. Although that number seems to be decreasing annually, the rate for unwed mothers is gradually increasing. "The number of combined children of divorce and children born to single mothers has continued to rise to 1,840,000 in 1980; 2,240,000 in 1990; 2,383,000 in 2000 and stood at an all time high of 2,661,000 in 2007."[5]

Although these statistics are jarring and heartbreaking, the sin that drives them has been in the hearts of men and women since the beginning. Of course, the prevalence of divorce has grown statistically in modern days because it is no longer considered an unacceptable solution to marital difficulties. In former times, a woman would have no means of support if she were not cared for by her father or husband, unless she became a prostitute. Although divorce was not as financially devastating for a man, he would suffer a social stigma that would follow him into all of his business dealings. Leaving a legacy for one's children and raising them to be contributing members of society was considered the primary goal of the family; a man would be labeled as dishonorable if he deserted his children.

The laws of the land reflected this emphasis, and divorces were far more difficult to obtain in the past. In fact, until the late 1960s it was very difficult to obtain a divorce; the petitioner would have to prove that the other party had broken the marital contract in order for a divorce to be granted. Of course, there were cases when this law was used to oppress the weak, but it did make the dissolution of the contract of marriage much more difficult. Now "no-fault" divorce—a divorce citing "irreconcilable differences"—is available in all fifty states, and the statistics and devastation wrought upon the family are obvious.

Yes, divorce is rampant in our country. You and your children will come in contact with someone who has been divorced or is in the middle of a divorce. There is just no way around it. Although divorce rates have dropped recently, marriage rates have dropped significantly more. Every year fewer people decide to get married at all. They may have been a victim of divorce or watched their parents divorce and are not willing to subject themselves to that pain again, so they decide a marriage contract is worthless. There are a variety of social, economic, psychological, physical, and spiritual effects that divorce can have on a person.

In this chapter we will review what the Bible says about marriage, divorce, remarriage, and adultery. Then we will get into the painful subject of talking to kids about these sad topics.

From the Beginning

God's original design for marriage was for it to be between one man and one woman for life. When questioned about why God allowed divorce in the law of Moses, Jesus said, "Because of your hardness of heart Moses allowed you to divorce your wives, but from the beginning it was not so" (Matthew 19:8). The relationship was to be sacred, set apart—a commitment made to God, to each other, and before witnesses. Each image bearer in marriage was to love and respect the partner, living in an unselfish way and subjugating the gratification of desires to the good of the family and ultimately the culture. This was God's design from the beginning, and then our hearts were hardened against him, against one another.

What causes divorces? Hard hearts.

Going back to the fall of man, we see the beginning of the degradation of the relationship between the man and his wife and their Lord. Eve blamed God's creation, Adam blamed God for giving him Eve, and the image of God in man and woman was shattered. In light of this history, it is no wonder we wound and divorce each other. We are shattered people married to shattered people, pursuing shattered dreams. But as we have seen before, the theme of the Bible never leaves us with the fall. Jesus came to redeem marriage, to show us what true love is like and forever transform how we look at the marriage relationship.

Understanding Marriage

Marriage is so much more than a sexual union. It is the commitment made before God and others to be joined for life (Matthew 19:4–6; Romans 7:1–3). God is intimately involved in each marriage union that takes place. In Malachi 2:14–15, God is said to witness this covenant. And in this same passage we also see that God joins the two individuals together in a remarkable way: "Did he not make them one, with a portion of the Spirit in their union?"

Jesus himself reiterates God's respect of marriage and commends it for a lifetime:

> Have you not read that he who created them from the beginning made them male and female, and said, "Therefore a man shall leave his father and his mother and hold fast to his wife, and the two shall become one flesh"? So they are no longer two but one flesh. What therefore God has joined together let not man separate.
>
> Matthew 19:4–6

The *ESV Study Bible* clarifies this passage:

God has joined together implies that marriage is not merely a human agreement but a relationship in which God changes the status of a man and a woman from being single (**they are no longer two**) to being married (**one flesh**). From the moment they are married, they are unified in a mysterious way that belongs to no other human relationship, having all the God-given rights and responsibilities of marriage that they did not have before.[6]

In Ephesians 5, we see that marriage concerns more than just a man and a woman in relationship. Marriage is a picture of the relationship between Christ and his bride, the church: "This mystery is profound, and I am saying that it refers to Christ and the church" (v. 32). Marriage is to reflect Christ's relationship with the church. The husband is to love as Christ has loved, by laying down his life. The wife is to submit as the church submits to Christ, fully resting in and assured of his love and committed to his purposes. God's steadfast covenant love for his people is displayed in Hosea 2:19–20:

> And I will betroth you to me forever. I will betroth you to me in righteousness and in justice, in steadfast love and in mercy. I will betroth you to me in faithfulness. And you shall know the Lord.

In these verses we see that marriage is to be for life. We also see the heart of a gracious Savior who loves us deeply and doesn't want us to think of him as a distant relative, or a harsh judge, or even just a good friend. Rather, he is to be our beloved, our Husband. Truly he views us as his beloved. He is jealous for our love in return.

Divorce

There are some cases in which it is biblically acceptable to divorce. It was never God's intention that a marriage should end in divorce, but people are broken sinners. In both the Old and New Testament, God allowed divorce in order to protect and help people who are faced with difficult situations. Once again we can return to Jesus' conversation with the Pharisees in Matthew 19:

> Because of your hardness of heart Moses allowed you to divorce your wives, but from the beginning it was not so. And I say to you: whoever divorces his wife, except for sexual immorality, and marries another, commits adultery.
>
> vv. 8–9

Jesus does not say divorce is always allowable. He does not allow it just because we feel like we don't love our spouse anymore or because we think we've found someone who really understands us and with whom we feel more compatible. The Bible clearly states that divorce always has its genesis in a hardening of the heart. It begins in a rebellion toward God (Matthew 5:27–30; 15:19; James 1:14–15) on the part of one or perhaps both of the spouses. Anytime a divorce takes place, something other than the spouse and devotion to God has taken priority in the marriage. Even good things can take wrong priority. Perhaps our children, job, parents, friends, or even the church has become more important than they should be. So it is in our relationship with God. Whenever anything takes priority over devotion to him or takes our affections away from God and to something else, we then "cheat on" God (James 4:4–5).

Adultery

Jesus cites adultery as one of the two grounds for divorce. That is because adultery is a serious offense against God; it shatters the covenant promise to be one flesh with the other. Adultery has lifelong consequences, even if the offense is forgiven. It flows from a heart that is idolatrous, and though that sounds terrible, each of our hearts is capable of this sin, given the right circumstances. We must be vigilant and guard what belongs only to our spouse, for we are one flesh, joined by our Creator. Ultimately, though, we must be enraptured with the love of God for us in Christ. This is the only love that will keep our hearts enthralled for a lifetime.

I am sure there are people who are reading this right now who have been wounded by a spouse's adultery or have even committed adultery. If that is you, please hear that God's grace is far deeper than any wound committed against you or any sin you have committed. There is real sin and real pain in this world, but we have a real Savior who takes all of our pain and sin and shame upon himself, forgives us, and dresses us in his righteousness alone. He is forever the faithful Spouse. He is our beloved and we are his.

Marriage to an Unbeliever

Paul gives us one other biblical reason for divorce in 1 Corinthians 7:12–15:

> To the rest I say (I, not the Lord) that if any brother has a wife who is an unbeliever, and she consents to live with him, he should not divorce her. If any woman has a husband who is an unbeliever, and he consents to live with her, she should not divorce him. For the unbelieving husband is made holy because of his wife, and the unbelieving wife is made holy because of her husband. Otherwise your children would be unclean, but as it is, they are holy. But if the unbelieving partner separates, let it be so. In such cases the brother or sister is not enslaved. God has called you to peace.

The new Christians in Corinth were wondering about their marital status now that they had come to faith. Most of them were married to unbelievers and didn't know what they should do. Should they divorce their unbelieving spouses? Were their marriages valid? What about their children? Were they cursed because they had an unbelieving mother or father?

Paul wrote that if a believer is married to an unbeliever, and the unbeliever is content to stay in the marriage, the believer should not seek a divorce; he encouraged families to stay together. But he also writes that if the unbeliever decides he or she no longer wants to live with this person who has newly become a Christian, the believing spouse is to let the unbeliever go. God has set up a safety net for all those in this circumstance. We are not enslaved to stay in a marriage where the unbeliever wants to divorce. These verses do not say believers *must* divorce unbelievers, but rather that they are able to divorce biblically if they choose to. Paul adds, "For how do you know, wife, whether you will save your husband? Or how do you know, husband, whether you will save your wife?" (1 Corinthians 7:16). It may be a saving grace to the unbeliever for the believer to stay in the marriage. Any decision to divorce would have to be made after much prayer and counsel with church leaders.

Are There Other Biblical Grounds for Divorce?

There are many differing opinions as to whether sexual immorality and abandonment of the family by the unbeliever are the only two biblical reasons for divorce. Some people believe the following Bible passage also applies to a marriage: "If he takes another wife to himself, he shall not diminish her food, her clothing, or her marital rights. And if he does not do these three things for her, she shall go out for nothing, without payment of money" (Exodus 21:10–11). In this example from the case law in Exodus, provisions are made for the care of a Hebrew slave woman who has subsequently been taken in marriage by her master. If, after they marry, the master decides he doesn't like her any longer, he is still obligated to care for her, and if he doesn't provide as he should, she is free to leave his home and her indenture for free.

Some Christians read this passage to mean that at the very least a husband is obligated to provide food, clothing, and marital rights (sex). If these three things are not provided, the wife may leave the spouse. Arguing from the perspective that a Christian wife should have at least as much protection as a Hebrew slave, they allow the woman to divorce her husband if he refuses to work to provide for the needs of the household. In this case they say the husband is acting like an unbeliever (1 Timothy 5:8) who has in essence abandoned his family, even though he may not actually ever get up off the couch.

Other Christians believe there are absolutely no biblical grounds for divorce, even in the case of adultery or abandonment. Many churches differ in their views on this subject; you should seek to discover what your church believes, and then speak to your children about those beliefs.

Most Christians believe that men and women who have obtained a "righteous" divorce—a divorce pursued for biblical reasons—have the right to remarry. This remarriage is available not only for the widow, but also for those who have been abandoned through adultery or absence. Of course, any subsequent remarriage must always be under the care and counsel of your local church and only "in the Lord," that is, only to another believer.

Talking to Your Kids

Preschool

As with all conversations with preschool-age children, keep this discussion simple. A younger preschooler may not be able to understand what it would mean for a family to be changed forever.

> God made marriage. It was his idea. He said a man and a woman should promise to stay together for the rest of their lives. When people get married, God makes something special happen. He takes the two people and sort of sticks them together to make one person. Think of when you play with Legos and you take two pieces and put them together to make one piece. That is what God does with two people who get married. Sometimes, when a person does bad things, he or she hurts the person they are married to. Sometimes that hurt makes the other person not want to be with them anymore. When two people who are married decide not to be married anymore, they get a divorce. A divorce is when the mommy or daddy leaves the house where the kids live. It is very sad. God doesn't like divorce; it hurts everyone.

If you are talking about your own divorce, you could add the following lines that may apply to your situation.

> This is not your fault. Mommy and Daddy have made choices that have hurt you, and we are sorry. We both love you. I believe God will help us through this. In times when we don't understand what is happening, we can remember that he loves us, that he is strong, and that he knows the best way to help us.

Ages 5 to 10

At this age, kids will undoubtedly have friends who are from broken families. Again, you don't have to go into a lot of details yet. Keep this talk tailored to their age, maturity, and personality.

> God made marriage. Marriage is a very good thing. It is when a man and a woman promise to love and help each other for the

rest of their lives. They make that promise to each other and to God. When they make that promise, God does something very cool—he takes the two people and makes them into one. They are still two people, but in God's eyes and in their hearts they are one.

God loves marriage. God even talks about being married to us. He promises to be with us and love us forever. But there are times when married people hurt each other. Sometimes when they do really hurtful things they end up deciding that they don't want to be married anymore. This is called getting a divorce. Divorce is painful, not just for the mommy and daddy, but for the kids, too. Either the mom or the dad moves out of the home and they stop living together. God doesn't like divorce, but there are times when he says it is okay to divorce someone. God says it's okay for a husband or wife to divorce their partner if their partner decides that they love someone else and has given their heart to a new person instead of the one they promised to love forever. The Bible calls this adultery. It is a sin in God's eyes.

But just because a man or woman gives their heart to another person, it doesn't mean the married couple *has to* get a divorce. Sometimes they can forgive each other and stay married. There are lots of reasons why people get divorced, some of them the Bible says are okay and others the Bible says are not okay. The good news is we know God will take care of his children even if they do get divorced. The Bible tells us that God loves the brokenhearted, and that is what divorce causes: broken hearts. God's love is big enough and strong enough to heal broken hearts.

If you happen to be in the middle of a divorce, it is important for the kids to know that even if things are changing in the family, they can count on two things: First, God is lovingly overseeing everything and, second, you love them and will continue to love them no matter what. They also need to be reassured over and over that the divorce is not their fault. Be honest with them about what has happened, without sullying the other's reputation. We are all broken sinners in need of a great Savior. You don't need to minimize the pain of divorce, but you should seek to maximize the truth of the goodness of God and how he cares for us even during really difficult times.

Ages 11 and Up

Children of this age will have a greater understanding of the dissolution of relationship. They may have even experienced it themselves, with a friend or even a boyfriend or girlfriend.

Marriage was God's idea. When a man and a woman get married they are making a promise to God, to each other, and to their family and friends to love their spouse for the rest of their lives. God does something really special when people make this promise. He takes their words seriously and makes the two lives into one. Divorce is when two married people decide not to be married anymore. There are a lot of reasons people get divorced. The Bible talks about a few reasons that make divorce an okay thing to do. First, when one person gives his or her heart to someone else instead of to the one they are married to, it is called adultery and it is okay to divorce that person. When people commit adultery it is because they think that they need something other than God and their spouse to make them happy. The truth is, God's forever love is the only love that will always make us happy. Adultery hurts everybody. It doesn't just hurt the husband or wife who was cheated on, but it hurts the kids, and even friends of the couple. Every single one of us is capable of doing something this hurtful to people we love. The good news is that God's love is bigger and deeper than any hurt. Sometimes people decide to stay together even after one of them has committed adultery. God can do some pretty amazing things; he can take marriages that are broken and make them better.

Another reason the Bible says people can get divorced is when a believer (someone who loves God) is married to an unbeliever (someone who doesn't love God) and the unbeliever wants to leave the believer. In that case the believer can divorce the unbeliever. God loves us and wants peace for us, and even though divorce is painful and awful, he allows it in these circumstances. God also talks about how he is married to us, his people. He is trying to show us that he loves us like a husband loves his wife. He doesn't just love us in a far-off way, but he loves us dearly. God also promises to always be with us. He will never divorce us, no matter what we do.

Again, if you are going through a divorce, you will be able to go into more specifics with your children. Always remind them that it is not their fault, and that God can and does use everything for our good and for his glory. It is important not to slander your spouse, especially if it hurts that your children still love your spouse after your spouse hurt you so deeply. Children need both their father and their mother.

Of course, if your spouse is physically or sexually abusive, you should take immediate actions, such as involving your church leaders and calling the police and filing criminal charges to keep him or her away from you and your children. But if the divorce has occurred for other less serious reasons, you cannot keep your kids away from your spouse, and you shouldn't seek to undermine their relationship with their parent. As they grow and mature, they will see the things you see, but you should seek to be an example of what it means to love even your enemies.

In a Nutshell

- God ordained that marriages should last our entire lifetime.

- Because of the "hardness" of our hearts, God allows divorce.
- It is generally believed that he allows divorce for two reasons:
  - Marital infidelity
  - Abandonment by an unbelieving spouse
    - Some believe that if the husband fails to provide bare necessities for the family, he has abandoned the family and may be divorced.
- Divorce hurts everyone involved, but Jesus bears our sorrows and forgives our sins.

6

Why Does the Bible Say That? Difficult Bible Stories

Here are headlines from what might be a sleazy tabloid in a grocery store (but are actually found in the Bible):

- "Dad unknowingly has sex with daughter-in-law! (She pretends to be a prostitute!)" (Genesis 38)

- "War hero makes foolish vow! Returning veteran promises to sacrifice the first thing he sees after his deployment. It's his daughter." (Judges 11)

- "Drunkenness and incest! Daughters seduce their drunken father so they can have children." (Genesis 19:30–38)

- "Jealousy, kidnapping, and lies! Jealous brothers sell their younger brother into slavery and tell their father he was killed by a wild animal." (Genesis 37)

- "Beautiful woman kidnapped by a king! Her husband told her to lie and say she was his sister!" (Genesis 12)

- "Sex and murder! A king with many wives sees another man's wife and forces her to have sex with him. When it is discovered she is pregnant, he arranges her husband's death!" (2 Samuel 11)

- "Sex with his dad's mistress!" (Genesis 35:21–22)

- "Couple die on church floor! Husband and wife sell their home, lie to their pastor about the amount of the proceeds, and are struck dead for it." (Acts 5:1–11)

- "Racist used by God! Man is commanded to tell people he hates about God. He acquiesces, but when the people repent and believe, he is angry and begs God to kill him because he hates them so much." (Jonah)

- "Man known for his great wisdom foolishly has 700 wives and 300 concubines!" (1 Kings 11:1–3)

- "A murderer becomes deliverer and questions God's power!" (Exodus 2, 4)

- "Gang rape, murder, and horrifying mail! A visitor to a city is accosted by men who demand to have sex with him. Instead, he gives them his concubine and they rape her until she dies. The visitor cuts up his concubine into twelve pieces and sends them to the people of the land." (Judges 19)

- "It's the end (almost)! The entire earth is flooded and everything dies except one man and his family." (Genesis 6–8)

- "You call him a king? At his death, Christ's closest friends sleep, commit an act of violence, betray, deny, and desert him." (Matthew 26)

That's quite a list, isn't it? Gang rape, murder, slavery, polygamy, adultery, treachery, and deceit fill the pages of the Bible. When you and your children read the Bible, it is easy to become confused—especially if you read your Bible in the wrong way.

How Should We Interpret These Stories?

How do we explain these stores to our children? How do we interpret the messes we see in the Bible in light of our innate desire for a tidy, pristine religion? When I read the stories mentioned above, I am sickened, confused, and troubled. I would imagine you are, too.

To understand why these stories would even make it into the Bible, we need to learn how to read God's Word. Too many of us think the Bible is a moral guidebook on how to be better people. If we think the Bible is sort of a glorified Aesop's fables—nice stories with an obvious moral, meant to encourage us to be better people—then these stories will make no sense. Where is the moral? Who are we supposed to be like? Where is the hero?

Sally Lloyd-Jones helps us understand the right way to interpret the Bible in her excellent *Jesus Storybook Bible*:

> Now, some people think the Bible is a book of rules, telling you what you should and shouldn't do. The Bible certainly does have some rules in it. They show you how life works best. But the Bible isn't mainly about you and what you should be doing. It's about God and what he has done. Other people think the Bible is a book of heroes, showing you people you should copy. The Bible does have some heroes in it, but (as you'll soon find out) most of the people in the Bible aren't heroes at all. They make some big mistakes (sometimes on purpose), they get afraid and run away. At times they are downright mean. No, the Bible isn't a book of rules, or a book of heroes. The Bible is most of all a Story. It's an adventure story about a young Hero who comes from a far country to win back his lost treasure. It's a love story about a brave Prince who leaves his palace, his throne—everything—to rescue the one he loves. It's like the most wonderful of fairy tales that has come true in real life.[1]

The troubling stories we referenced at the beginning of this chapter are just a taste of the many disturbing narratives found in the Bible. They force us to think more deeply about the Bible and teach us to see it as more than a superficial story about sweet people who lived tidy lives. It is a realistic depiction of the desperate condition of the human race. It isn't a book about perfect people making flawless decisions and reaping the reward for their perfections. It is a book that ultimately points to the one perfect Person who made every decision in righteousness and then was punished for all of our imperfections.

The Bible Probably Isn't What We Think It Is

The Bible (and Christianity) is counterintuitive. Think of it: Most religions put their best foot forward. They showcase the people who make their religion look best. They only mention kings who are strong and capable, and only talk about the leading men as those who never doubted, never messed up, and always came out on top. Christianity takes that model and completely flips it on its dishonest head. The Bible shows us what people are really like. It paints a picture that demonstrates how desperate humanity is. Even our "fathers in the faith," such as Abraham and David, had serious problems.

This true-to-life portraiture is one characteristic that makes the Bible unique and Christianity different. It doesn't ignore the ugly history of man but rather takes hold of it, owns it, and gives us a Savior who will come and make everything right. This gives us hope, because on the days when we don't even want to read our Bible, let alone talk to our kids about it, we can rest in the knowledge that God is not surprised by our failure.

There will be days when we doubt there really is a God who loves us and we can't even remember why we believe

Christianity is true. It is on those days the Holy Spirit will remind us of Peter, who denied Christ and yet was still welcomed and loved. On those days we can remember David, the adulterous murderer who was called "a man after God's own heart." We can think of Abraham, who forced Sarah to lie about being his wife and yet is called the father of our faith (Romans 4:12).

The Bible eases our troubled hearts so that we can fully embrace our humanity, and it leads us to see our desperate need for a Redeemer. These Bible stories force us to look outside of weak humanity for the help we need. We see that all people are wicked and selfish and that it took God himself to come and live the life we needed to live, and to die the death reserved for wicked people like us.

Learning How to Interpret God's Word

Pastor and teacher Bryan Chapell suggests we ask ourselves two questions when reading the Bible. First, "What does this text reflect about the nature of God who provides redemption?" and second, "What does this text reflect about the nature of humanity that requires redemption?" He explains:

> These simple questions are the lenses to the reading glasses through which we can look at any text to see what the Bible is reflecting of God's nature and/or human nature. Inevitably these lenses enable us to see that God is holy and we are not, or that God is sovereign and we are vulnerable, or that God is merciful and we require his mercy. Such reading glasses always make us aware of our need of God's grace to compensate for our sin and inability. Christ may not be specifically mentioned in the text, but the reflection of God's nature and ours makes the necessity of his grace apparent.

Using these reading glasses throughout the Old and New Testament will enable us to see the gracious nature of God who provides redemption as he gives strength to the weak, rest to the weary, deliverance to the disobedient, faithfulness to the unfaithful, food to the hungry and salvation to sinners. We also learn something about the human nature that requires redemption when heroes fail, patriarchs lie, kings fall, prophets cower, and covenant people become idolaters. These lenses prevent us from setting up characters in the Bible *only* as moral heroes to emulate, rather than as flawed men and women who themselves needed the grace of God.

Every text, seen in its redemptive context, is reflecting an aspect of humanity's fallen condition that requires the grace of God. Focus upon this fallen condition will inevitably cause readers to consider the divine solution characteristic of the grace that culminates in the provision of the Savior.[2]

The Lord's inclusion of these troubling stories in the Bible by no means denotes approval of them. We must not presume that because they are in the Bible God sees nothing wrong with them; nor should we accept them as normative behavior, either. At times they are troubling, not because the behavior is so outrageous but because we aren't given a tidy outcome.

These Stories Give Us Hope

Think for a moment about Jonah, a racist sent to the very people he hated. We would like to see repentance at the end of his story. We want to see that Jonah's heart was changed and moved with love for the Ninevites. Instead, Jonah's last spoken words are, "Yes, I do well to be angry, angry enough to die" (Jonah 4:9). Why does God end Jonah's story there? Why isn't he a transformed man? Because the Bible presents a realistic view of humanity. There are times people don't change, or their change is painfully slow. We are meant to see that God's covenant love for his people is not dependent on our change; it is dependent on his heart. It is dependent on his pursuing love—a love for a racist. He pursues the unlovable.

The truth about God's love smashes our idol of wanting a hero and of wanting to be a hero. People are deeply flawed and have been since nearly the beginning of time. Every single Bible story that is disturbing or unpleasant shows us that fact in black and white. If this were the whole story it would be utterly depressing. But the story doesn't end there. It ends with the most vividly beautiful display of God's love for us in Christ. Every time we see the need for redemption, we can also see that God doesn't leave us in our failure and misery. God rescues us. He sent his Son into this ghastly world full of disgusting sin. The pure, spotless Lamb of God—the One who had never experienced anything but pure holiness—came to us, the ones who know only wickedness. This Lamb of God experienced the pain of rejection, the ache of losing a parent and friends in death, the sting of betrayal by those who should have loved and supported him. When common sense would say, "Judge them and leave them to themselves," Love incarnate says, "Go to them, be all that they can't be, and then lay down your life to bring them into our family."

These stories are not included to make light of, minimize, or glorify sin. These stories are told so that we can see the sickening and terrifying effects sin has on humanity. These stories are told to make us hate sin. They also show us that no man is beyond God's grace. The vilest sinner can be accepted into the priesthood of believers, for no matter how vile the sin, the grace of God is greater.

Let's determine to be honest with our kids about our doubts as we read these Bible stories. If the story is confusing to you, tell them that. There is no point in hiding; we can be honest and look for answers together.

Talking to Your Kids

Preschool

Most children in this age range won't understand the graphic and troubling nature of certain Bible stories. Some stories are not even appropriate for young children to hear about. Let me encourage you to simply guard their little minds. You don't need to expose them to every difficult narrative in the Old Testament. If they do have questions about something you have read together or something they heard, you can just point them back to what you know about God.

> There are stories in the Bible that are hard to understand. When we hear these stories, we can remember what we know about God. Remembering what God is like helps us all the time. God is loving, powerful, and wise. Some stories in the Bible are there just to show us how much people need a Rescuer. Sometimes stories are in the Bible to show us how good God is at being our Rescuer. People do and say really sad and hurtful things, but God is the best at healing and helping.

If your children have questions that go deeper than what is covered above, you could always study particular Bible stories and see what more you can glean and share with them.

Ages 5 to 10

Children in this age group might be exposed to more of these stories. Wisdom would dictate that they are still too young to absorb the awful state of the human condition. So, once again, we would encourage you to emphasize what God and people are like. If your children are mature enough, you could teach them a bit about how to read their Bibles, too.

> The Bible is not a book about the best people in all of history. The Bible is a true story about how our God used some of the worst people in history to make himself look amazing. The Bible isn't just a book that tells you how to live and what you should and shouldn't do. The reason we have the Bible is so we can learn about how perfect Jesus was and how much God loves his people. There are some really icky stories in the Bible. It is good they are there, because we know God loves even the worst of the worst people. His love and forgiveness are so big that he can take someone who has done something terrible and love them into his family. This really is good news because a lot of times both you and I do stuff that is pretty terrible, too. Some stories in the Bible are there to show us how great this love is and how strong and powerful God is. Some stories are in the Bible to show us how much people need a strong, wise, and loving God to come and rescue them. There are going to be things you don't understand in the Bible, and that is okay. There are things I don't understand, either. God doesn't ask us to believe perfectly, he just asks us to have faith the size of a mustard seed. A mustard seed is very, very small. When we read or hear a story we don't understand, we can just remember what we already know about God, and ask him to help us understand. The problem is that our minds are kind of tricky and sometimes we don't think quite right, but God loves us through that, too.

Ages 11 and Up

As children grow and mature in their understanding of life, they will grow in their understanding of how shocking some Bible stories are. We must not belittle them for their questions or bully them into believing. It is very common for children in this age group to start to wonder if the Bible is true and if God is real. It is okay to talk them through their questions, pray for them, and leave the rest in our heavenly Father's hands. Doubting is not necessarily a sign of spiritual distress. It could be they are truly trying to reconcile what they believe with what they see and hear. David expressed doubt in several psalms. In Psalm 10:1 he cried out, "Why, O Lord, do you stand far away? Why do you hide yourself in times of trouble?"

We see how kindly and patiently the Lord responds to doubt as we observe his interaction with the disciples after his resurrection:

> As they were talking about these things, Jesus himself stood among them, and said to them, "Peace to you!" But they were startled and frightened and thought they saw a spirit. And he said to them, "Why are you troubled, and why do doubts arise in your hearts? See my hands and my feet, that it is I myself. Touch me, and see. For a spirit does not have flesh and bones as you see that I have." And when he had said this, he showed them his hands and his feet. And while they still disbelieved for joy and were marveling, he said to them, "Have you anything here to eat?" They gave him a piece of broiled fish, and he took it and ate before them.
>
> Luke 24:36–43

Jesus bears with their weaknesses. We often think it was just Thomas who doubted, but in fact it was all the disciples. The news of a resurrected Savior is so glorious, so unbelievable, that doubting it is a normal response. Thomas was not present at this first interaction Jesus had with his disciples, yet once again we see Jesus having compassion on their frail minds. Most of us would have treated Thomas like he was an infidel or an idiot, maybe even cut him off from being a follower, but instead, our sweet Savior entreats him and loves him in his unbelief.

> Now Thomas, one of the Twelve, called the Twin, was not with them when Jesus came. So the other disciples told him, "We have seen the Lord." But he said to them, "Unless I see in his hands the mark of the nails, and place my finger into the mark of the nails, and place my hand into his side, I will never believe."
>
> Eight days later, his disciples were inside again, and Thomas was with them. Although the doors were locked, Jesus came and stood among them and said, "Peace be with you." Then he said to Thomas, "Put your finger here, and see my hands; and put out your hand, and place it in my side. Do not disbelieve, but believe." Thomas answered him, "My Lord and my God!" Jesus said to him, "Have you believed because you have seen me? Blessed are those who have not seen and yet have believed."
>
> John 20:24–29

Those who were closest to Jesus, those who had witnessed his beautiful life and shocking death, couldn't believe the truth that he had risen. How much more difficult is it for our children and us to believe? Yet Jesus has a word for all who believe without seeing him: He calls us blessed. Do not doubt that Jesus has the same patience with your child and with you as he did with Thomas. He knows our frame; remembers that we are dust (Psalm 103:14). He bears with us, even in our times of doubting.

When Your Children Doubt

Professor Jerram Barrs says this about children who doubt or have difficult questions about the Bible:

> When we take doubts seriously it encourages a young person to see that Christianity is indeed the truth, that it is not afraid

of the hard questions, but rather can stand up to any challenge. This builds confidence in the Lord and in His Word, preparing the young person for the trials ahead that life invariably brings. Throughout life people will ask hard questions. Because the Christian faith is the truth, because this Word is the truth, you can take those questions seriously no matter how hard they are, and you can answer them out of compassion and love.[3]

As you deal with your child's questions, you could say something like this:

> I understand you have doubts. If I am being honest, there are times I have doubts, too. The amazing thing about Christianity is that Jesus never says you have to believe perfectly or to never have any doubt. Jesus does tell us to believe in him, but he also says we are forgiven for the times we don't. He shows us that being honest about our doubts isn't a bad thing. He healed the son of the man who confessed his weak faith. The truth is, Jesus isn't concerned about the strength of your faith; he knows that what is important is the strength of the One on whom your faith rests. He is strong enough, loving enough, and gentle enough to take even the weakest faith and hide that person in his perfect faith.

As you talk to your children about troubling Bible stories, you could communicate these sentiments in a way that is understandable to them:

> There are some pretty unbelievable stories in the Bible—stories that are not only hard to understand, but also very troubling. When we read the Bible, we must do so with two different things in mind. First, we read the Bible to see how amazing God is. We see how strong he is at rescuing people—at rescuing sinners. The whole Bible points to the day when Jesus Christ did the ultimate

work of rescuing us. He did this when he died on the cross and rose from the dead. We must understand that the Bible isn't just a book about how to be a better person. The Bible is a book that tells us there is only one good Person. The second way we need to read our Bibles is to see how desperately everyone in history needs this strong Savior. The Bible includes some pretty terrible stories about pretty terrible people doing really terrible things. The beautiful part is, God uses these terrible people to build his family. If God didn't use terrible people, we would all be in a seriously bad situation. I don't always understand everything I read in the Bible, but I do know the God we serve. His ways are not our ways. We won't always have clear understanding. That is probably a good thing, because if you could understand God, he wouldn't be all that special. In our times of doubting, we can turn to him and know he won't be angry with us. He knows our minds, he knows our hearts, and he loves us and pursues us anyway.

In a Nutshell

- The Bible paints an honest picture of the sin of mankind.

- Just because a story is in the Bible, it doesn't mean God approves of it or condones it.

- The Bible is not like Aesop's fables. Bible stories are not given so we can be more like the characters in them.

- There is only one Hero in the Bible who we should want to be like.

- The stories in the Bible should lead us to ask two questions:

  · What does this story tell me about the nature of God who supplies redemption?

- What does this story tell me about the nature of man who requires redemption?
- Stories that show us how terrible mankind is also show us how great God's grace is.
- Sometimes these stories can make us doubt. Doubt is not sin. God will help us when we doubt.

7

Why and How
Do Some People Sin Sexually?

In this chapter we will discuss the horrific nature of some of
the most distressing sexual sins. Although we want to preserve
our children's sexual innocence, the truth is that our culture is
inundated with sex. In books, television, and especially on the
Internet, our young people are being exposed to sexual images
in a way unheard of just a generation ago. In one survey, when
researchers asked college students about their experience with
online pornography, a staggering 93 percent of boys and 62
percent of girls said they had seen Internet porn *before* the age
of eighteen.[1]

In light of this new reality, a parent's awkwardness or fear
of talking about sex with their children must be overcome. If
we refuse these discussions because we are self-conscious, feel
guilt for past failure, or are simply lazy, we force them to look
elsewhere to find answers. Even so, when we seek to protect
our children or when we strive to make sure we create a safe

environment for them, we cannot assume our protection will stop them from finding a way to seek information or from a perpetrator finding them. Boys and girls as young as nine years old are searching the Internet for answers to their sexually related questions.

The Way God Intended It

Early in the Bible we learn the Lord had a specific plan in mind for our sexuality: "And the man and his wife were both naked and were not ashamed" (Genesis 2:25). But then sin entered, and everything that had been right became very wrong: "So when the woman saw that the tree was good for food, and that it was a delight to the eyes, and that the tree was to be desired to make one wise, she took of its fruit and ate, and she also gave some to her husband who was with her, and he ate. Then the eyes of both were opened, and they knew that they were naked. And they sewed fig leaves together and made themselves loincloths" (Genesis 3:6–7).

In these three verses we see the degradation of sexuality. First, we see the way God intended us to live. We were to be so consumed with God—with so little thought of ourselves—that we could be naked and unashamed. Adam and Eve were so secure in God's love for them and their identity in him that there was no thought of how they looked to each other; it simply wouldn't have occurred to them to notice what they were (or were not) wearing.

Sexual union was beautiful and was all about pleasing the other person and rejoicing in God's good gift of pleasure. Tellingly, immediately after Adam and Eve sinned, they were aware of their nakedness. They tried to hide, to cover themselves. Sexuality became something we had to hide and something that belongs to only us. Professor and author Justin Holcomb writes,

Post fall, however, nudity became sheer vulnerability. More than polite embarrassment, shame implied the danger of physical exploitation and humiliation. We see this as Adam's shame soon festers into Noah's exploitation. Nakedness and exploitation mark the earliest characters in Genesis and are traced throughout as a symbol of the depth of the effects of sin.[2]

In the beginning, marriage was to be between "male and female" (Genesis 1:27). Adam and Eve's job was to "be fruitful and multiply and fill the earth" (Genesis 1:28). Sexual intimacy between married couples is a good gift from a good God. The point of being fruitful and multiplying was not only to procreate, but also to enjoy intimacy through each other's bodies (Proverbs 5:15–19; Song of Solomon; 1 Corinthians 7:2–5).

Adam and Eve's sin and resultant shame still has a devastating impact on our sexuality today. Once intended for mutual pleasure and intimacy, now sex is often used as a means to hurt and humiliate. Not only do we mar the beauty of sexuality by hurting and shaming others, we also distort the original plan for sexual union.

The Distortion

When Adam and Eve told God his love and covenant were not enough to fulfill them, the distortion of all good things began. God clearly said man was supposed to be with woman—as one who would be able to fulfill his need for a helper (Genesis 2:18). She was to help him rule over the creation and give birth to other children who would "fill the earth" (Genesis 1:28).

And the rib that the Lord God had taken from the man he made into a woman and brought her to the man. Then the man said, "This at last is bone of my bones and flesh of my flesh; she shall be called Woman, because she was taken out of Man." Therefore a man shall leave his father and his mother and hold fast to his wife, and they shall become one flesh.

Genesis 2:22–24

These two individuals were meant to be one flesh; the two parts were to be joined to make a whole. But that's not what we see around us now, is it? Since the fall, the meaning and purpose of our sexuality has changed. Now we hear "Do whatever feels good," and "Whatever happens behind closed doors doesn't hurt anybody else." We are forced to teach our children about safe sex because so many diseases are now transmitted through the sexual act; an act that was created innocent and pure has become the source of disease and death to millions.

Sexual sin is part of our depraved state. Galatians 5:19 says, "Now the works of the flesh are evident: sexual immorality, impurity, sensuality"; it is one of "the works of darkness" (Romans 13:12) and one of the reasons the wrath of God is coming (Colossians 3:6). Like all sin, it flows out from our own hearts and is not necessarily a side effect of poor parenting or a bad environment (Matthew 5:19; Mark 7:21–22). It does not merely affect the one committing the sin, it also affects all of society, as Paul demonstrates in his instructions to the church in Corinth where a man was having sex with his father's wife. Paul chastised the church, saying that they were proud and they should have removed the man from their fellowship because a little leaven leavens the whole lump (1 Corinthians 5:6). God hates sexual immorality and will bring judgment on those who sin sexually (Malachi 3:5; Jeremiah 13:26–27).

Homosexuality

During a family trip to Disneyland, my daughter, who was nine at the time, saw two men being affectionate with each other.

Needless to say, she was confused and wanted to know why they were acting that way. I told her they were homosexuals—that they were men who looked at other men in the same way Daddy and Mommy looked at each other. I told her homosexuality was sin, and like all other sin, it begins in our hearts, when we love something more than we love God. I told her that even though the men's sin seemed particularly wrong or different, before God, all sin is the same (Romans 6:23). All sin, whether culturally acceptable or not, is punishable before a holy God.

As my daughter struggled with this concept, I told her that sometimes I think the only thing that will make me happy is a quiet, clean house and a good book. During those times, I get angry with my kids when they interrupt my reading or make a mess. Ultimately I sin in order to get what I think will make me happy. Then I told her that in God's eyes homosexuality is just like that—that it is sin because some people think the only way they can be happy or feel loved is to be with a person of the same sex. I tried to stress the fact that we are sinners just like they are; their sin is no more punishable before a holy God than ours.

Then I told her that Jesus had to die for every kind of sin: for those that seem very acceptable and for those that seem very different. She looked at me with a concerned expression and said, "It seems like their sin is a lot worse. It just doesn't seem the same." It was so interesting that she came to that conclusion, because most Christians probably agree. While homosexuality is a sin that has devastating social consequences, before a holy God it is no more serious than anything festering in each of our hearts right now.

Homosexual sex is clearly and repeatedly prohibited in the Bible. Leviticus 18:22 says, "You shall not lie with a male as with a woman; it is an abomination." Again in Leviticus 20:13

we read, "If a man lies with a male as with a woman, both of them have committed an abomination." And then the ultimate indictment is found in Romans 1:26–27:

> For this reason God gave them up to dishonorable passions. For their women exchanged natural relations for those that are contrary to nature; and the men likewise gave up natural relations with women and were consumed with passion for one another, men committing shameless acts with men and receiving in themselves the due penalty for their error.

Homosexuality is sin, but it is not the unforgivable sin.[3] Wise parents should teach their children that all sin is idolatry and rebellion before God—and that they and their children should seek to love and serve those who are struggling with same-sex attraction, just as they seek to love those who make heterosexual relationships their god. And while some in the homosexual community are trying to silence the voice of the church, perhaps their response to the Christian community is in response to the condemnation they have felt from us. Jesus came to "seek and to save the lost" (Luke 19:10), and that includes hopeless wanderers who are struggling with any form of sexual deviancy.[4]

We must learn for ourselves and teach our children how to love these men and women without alienating them or pushing them deeper into their isolation, while at the same time not condoning their choices. Remembering that Jesus loves us without condoning our sin will be helpful in this process. We are called to love sinners just as he did.

There is a question of whether homosexuals are "born that way." In one sense, the answer is yes, because each of us sins and is "by nature [a child] of wrath" (Ephesians 2:3). We are born sinners. But we are also unique individuals, with a unique propensity to sin in a particular way, depending on what we love and desire most. Some of this has to do with our genes, some of it with our environment, most of it with our idols. Some of us are prone to lying, others gluttony, still others to anger. We are all prone to self-righteousness, so, yes, each one of us has his or her own particular weakness to fight against. But even if there is an inborn predisposition toward same-sex attraction, Paul teaches us that our sinful desires can be resisted in the name of the Lord and by the power of the Spirit:

> Do not be deceived: neither the sexually immoral, nor idolaters, nor adulterers, nor men who practice homosexuality . . . will inherit the kingdom of God. [Here's the good news] And *such were some of you.* But you were washed, you were sanctified, you were justified in the name of the Lord Jesus Christ and by the Spirit of our God.
>
> 1 Corinthians 6:9–11

The gospel is powerful enough to transform every heart, no matter our predilections. The love of God and free grace of Christ is to be demonstrated to all those who will hear us. A heart of compassion and understanding of the deceitfulness of sin will make us fervent to love and be patient with those who are struggling to be free.

Sexual Abuse

Alarmingly, statistics tell us that one out of every four girls and one out of every six boys is sexually abused by the time they are eighteen; most sexual abuse is perpetrated by a person whom a child is comfortable with and knows.[5] This is another one of those topics that we hate to talk about with our kids. It is uncomfortable and sad, but we must be open with them about this horrible sin.

Sexual abuse in the church is rampant. Predators know the church is a place where children are very trusting. I once heard that it is not a matter of *if* sexual abuse will happen in your church but *when*. This problem is not confined to large churches or small ones; it is a problem with depraved, wicked people who prey on the most unsuspecting, weak victims.

It is important to talk to your children about the dangers of sexual abuse. Explain to them, using anatomically correct language, that people may try to hurt them. The idea is not to instill a crippling fear but rather a realistic understanding so they can be aware of their surroundings and situations. They need to be comfortable talking to you about possible problems, and know that it is not their fault if they were sexually abused. Kids must know you will take their claim seriously and report the sexual abuse to the police. Too many times kids tell their parents about abuse and the parents try to fix the problem without getting authorities involved. The problem is, most sexual abusers are repeat offenders, so even if they don't abuse your child again, chances are they will abuse others. God has given us civil authorities to protect us and our children (1 Peter 2:13–14). It is irresponsible and ignorant not to report sexual abuse.

It is difficult to understand why someone would sexually abuse a child. Sexual abuse is not new. It was going on in Old Testament times; there are laws against rape found in Deuteronomy 22:25–27. We read about the rape of Tamar by her half-brother, Amnon, in 2 Samuel 13. God hates sexual abuse. Jesus' incarnation taught us the value of children because he himself was a child. So as horrible and disgusting as sexual abuse is, and as heartbreaking and detrimental as its effects are, we know that the God of the universe and his Son who loves us sympathize with our suffering. We know the powerful Holy Spirit works everything together to bring comfort and healing to victims.

Although sexual abuse is terrible, God's love and healing are bigger. The shame and guilt that come from sexual abuse can be overcome by the work of the Holy Spirit.

The isolation and loneliness abuse survivors feel can be answered in our sweet, compassionate Jesus who understands abuse, and in the church who weeps with them. Jesus himself was stripped naked and hung eye-level while haters walked by and spat on him, hurling insults. He felt the weight of being naked and ashamed, yet he endured this without sin and for our forgiveness.

I am sure there are abuse survivors reading this right now. May the love of Christ wash over you and cleanse you, may he restore what others have taken away, and may you find your identity in what he has done for you instead of what others have done to you.

Talking to Your Kids

Preschool

We have touched on two very troubling issues in this chapter. Hopefully you won't have to talk to preschoolers about homosexuality or sexual abuse, but it is important to talk to them about their bodies. The following paragraph comes from a friend who was very helpful to me in the writing of this book.

God made you. He made your body from your head to your toes. He made you strong and beautiful. He gave you to me, and my job as your mama (daddy) is to tell you that Jesus loves you always, no matter what. My other job is to love you and keep you safe. Your body is special and it belongs to you. You often like to be hugged and snuggled and tickled, but sometimes you don't want that. That's okay. You have the right to decide if you want to be touched or not. If you don't want to be touched or hugged or kissed, say "No, thank you." If the person doesn't listen, come tell me right away.

It is never okay for someone to touch your private parts. Your private parts are the body parts covered by a bathing suit. If anyone touches you there (on your vagina, breasts, bottom, or penis), come tell me. And if anyone touches you anywhere on your body (your head, your leg, your back . . .) and it makes you feel uncomfortable, scared, or just weird, let me know that, too. I'm so glad God made you and gave you to me. If you ever have any questions about your body or someone else's body, please come and talk to me. Other people's bodies belong to them, too, and it is wrong for you to touch their private parts. God made each of us in a special way, and he loves us.

Concerning Homosexuality

If a child who is preschool age doesn't ask about homosexuality, you don't need to engage her in a conversation about it. If she does, you can keep it very simple; you don't need to go into a lot of detail.

Everybody does things they think will make them happy. Sometimes you take toys that are not yours because you want to play with them and you think they will make you happy. You know that taking toys is wrong and that God tells you not to do it. God tells us that a man and a woman are made for each other, but some men think being in love with another man will make them happy, and some women think being in love with another woman will make them happy. We know that God's rules are best. He is the smartest. So we should follow God's rules. But even when we don't, and we do things we shouldn't, he forgives us and loves us anyway. God's love for us is better than any toy and better than the love of any other person. His love is the biggest, deepest love, and it is enough to make you happy.

Ages 5 to 10

This is a wide age range for this topic. You may want to keep the younger kids in the preschool age talk. Again, please know your child. Don't be afraid to ask him if he has ever been touched in a way that made him feel uncomfortable. Remind him that he will not be in trouble if that has happened to him. The amount of shame sexual abuse survivors feel can be crippling, so they need to be assured of your love.

God made your body. He made you perfectly the way he wanted you to be. He gave you special parts—your penis (or vagina and breasts). They are not meant to be touched by anybody else until you are married. Those special parts are yours alone. If anybody ever asks to see them or tries to touch them, you need to come and tell me. Or if somebody touches you somewhere else on your body that makes you feel uncomfortable, even if it is just your leg or your stomach, please come and tell me. It is my job to help you protect your body.

There are people who want to hurt children, and I want to keep you safe. If you are ever in a situation where you feel weird, it is okay just to walk or run away. You don't have to say why. You come straight to me and tell me that something happened that made you feel uncomfortable. It doesn't matter who the other person is, it doesn't matter if it seems rude, or if the person is an adult, you come to me. Sometimes your friends might want to touch you or see those special parts of your body. You can tell them no. Even if you are playing a game and they tell you it is part of the game, you can tell them no. If you are too embarrassed to say no, or you don't feel like you can say no to an adult or a friend, you can tell me afterward. You might feel really bad and feel like you did something wrong, but I promise I won't be angry with you. I love you and want to protect and help you. Jesus loves children. In the Bible he had some pretty strong words for people who hurt children. God loves to make sad things come untrue; he loves to take icky situations and turn them around. So please know that no matter what has happened in the past, God can help you and heal you.

CONCERNING HOMOSEXUALITY

Everybody does what they think will make them happy. Sometimes we do things we know are wrong if we think we will be happy. God tells us that a man and a woman were made for each other. Sometimes boys think they will be happy if they are with another boy, and girls think they will be happy if they are with another girl. I am not talking about friendships, but rather about being with someone like husbands are with their wives. It is important you don't ever shame somebody because of their sin, especially if we don't understand their sin. For homosexuals and for those who aren't homosexual but sin in other ways, Jesus had to die on the cross. He had to pay for each of our sins. Each of us looks for ways to make ourselves happy, and God tells us that he is the only One who will make us happy. Each one of us has certain temptations that pull on our hearts, telling us to go in an opposite way than God has told us. God promises to help us in our times of temptation, and he promises to forgive us when we give in to our temptations. His love is that big and that strong.

It is important to emphasize God's redemptive purposes in all of life. We don't want our kids to look down on homosexuals, but rather love them the way Christ has loved us.

Ages 11 and Up

PORNOGRAPHY

This is a section I didn't include in the younger age groups, but it is an important topic for kids in this age range. You must talk to your children about the dangers of pornography and why it is wrong. If you leave it unsaid, you can be assured they will hear about it from others, and even their own curiosity may possibly take them to the Internet.

> Looking at pornography is a dangerous sin. When you look at another person naked to make yourself feel good, you believe that God's love for you isn't enough. Porn isn't a safe way to explore sex. Not only does porn negatively affect you, but it also hurts others. You may think it is no big deal and you aren't sinning against anybody, but it does hurt large groups of people. The women and men who are in the pictures or the videos that you are looking at are real people who were created in the image of God. When you look at those images and use them for your pleasure, you are using others selfishly. You are living as though these people don't have real lives; they are just objects for you to look at. The people in these videos may be sex slaves—they may have been kidnapped or sold by their parents to people who force them to make Internet pornography. Other porn is made by people who are addicted to drugs or alcohol, and the people producing the porn make them work for drugs.
>
> Pornography destroys lives—not only the lives of people who made the porn but even those who look at it. Looking at pornography a lot can also damage your brain.[6] It will affect your future relationships because you will have the images of what you have seen burned into your memory and you will compare your future sexual relationship in marriage to what you watched. And although sex in marriage is wonderful, it is never like it is in pornography. That's because those people are acting. If you have already looked at pornography, even if it is a habit, there is hope for you. Jesus came to save prostitutes and sinners. He came to free us from our addictions by forgiving our sins and giving us his perfect record. He never looked at a woman in a

lustful way, and that is how God views you, if you believe and trust in him. Don't believe that your sin will hold God back from loving you, but also understand that your goodness won't make him love you any more. God loves you as he loves his Son.

HOMOSEXUALITY

This topic may be one of great confusion to preteens and teenagers. They are aware of what same-sex attraction is, and possibly may be experiencing it. They are also aware of the disgrace that comes with being a homosexual. They may have friends or acquaintances who are homosexuals, and they are not sure exactly how to treat them. We want to be sure they know what the Bible says about it, but we also want to shower grace upon those who struggle with the sin. We need to be open to talking to our kids about this and also to the possibility that this may be a struggle in their lives. Our stance needs to be one of love and hope, not one of condemnation and hate.

Homosexuality (an inappropriate sexual relationship with someone of your own gender) is wrong according to Scripture. We believe the Bible is our standard for all of life, and the Bible tells us that God's original design was for a man and woman to be together. Our culture either makes fun of homosexuals or it exalts them, but both of these responses are wrong. We shouldn't laugh at or hurt those who are in sin. There are many people who struggle with same-sex attraction and they hate it. Every time we make fun of them it pushes them further into their shame and hurts them, confirming in their minds that they are too different to ever be loved.

The other side is that lots of movies, television, and books look to exalt homosexuals. Society condemns Christians for speaking out against homosexuals and tells us to "do whatever feels right." This is contrary to Scripture, too, and although our hearts should hurt for those who struggle, we can't lie by saying God doesn't care about it. He does. He knows what is best for us and he asks us to obey.

You may wonder why some people are attracted to the same sex. We ultimately don't know the answer to that question. There may be a lot of different factors that contribute to the way they feel, but we know that ultimately God will help and love all sinners who come to him. He forgives every type of sin and loves us regardless of what we struggle with. We must have the same heart as our heavenly Father, one that welcomes and loves all types of people. Homosexual sin is like any other sin you struggle with. We don't need to separate ourselves from homosexuals or act like they are worse than we are. We are all in need of the death of Christ himself in order to be forgiven.

SEXUAL ABUSE

Sexual abuse is a sad, terrible sin that affects many people. There are people who hurt others to make themselves feel powerful or good. Sexual abuse isn't just when someone touches you inappropriately or makes you do something you don't want to do; sexual abuse can also be a boyfriend or a girlfriend convincing you to do something you don't want to do by manipulating you, or telling you that you have to prove your love for them. Sexual abuse often happens by those we trust the most. If it has happened to you, you don't need to feel ashamed. It is important to understand that it is not your fault if someone has hurt you. Even if the person who touched you blamed it on you and said it was your fault, it isn't. Sometimes an abuser will say you will get in trouble or that he will hurt you if you tell what he did. Don't believe him; he is lying. I promise to protect you from anyone who tries to hurt you, and I always want to hear if anything like this has ever or will ever happen. Even if you already made some bad decisions, and you were drunk or maybe someone drugged you, it is still not your fault and I want to know about it.

Sexual abuse is an awful part of a lot of people's stories, but it is not their whole story. God often takes the most terrible, ugly circumstances and changes them into beautiful stories of redemption. Jesus Christ understands the shame of sexual humiliation because he was hung naked at his crucifixion and was taunted by those passing by. In your deepest humiliation and shame, Christ knows and feels for you. He prays for you. We are never alone in our suffering. You have a new identity in Christ. He does not view people who have been sexually abused as damaged and of no worth. Rather, they are loved by God and welcomed as pure and undefiled just as Christ is. Our identity is completely hidden in who Christ is and what he has done. We have all sinned against others and been sinned against by others, but what Jesus has done covers it all. He forgives us, he restores us, and he welcomes us.

In a Nutshell

- Sexual deviation and sin is rampant in our culture and even in our churches.
- In the beginning, God created the sexual union as a means not only of procreation but also as a source of pleasure.
- Sexual intimacy is meant for one man and one woman for life in marriage.
- Sin ruined this relationship and introduced shame.
- Homosexuality is sin, but it is not the unforgivable sin.
- Sexual abuse is widespread, even in the church.
- Jesus died to save sinners, even those who have sinned sexually.

8

Why Does God Let Natural Disasters Happen?

A s I sit down to write this chapter, the news is full of stories about a series of tornadoes that have wreaked havoc on Oklahoma. One twister was 2.6 miles wide at one point and produced wind speeds up to 265 mph. The death toll now stands at twenty people, including six children. Earlier this spring, another tornado swept through Moore, Oklahoma, and hit an elementary school. Seven children were thrown into a nearby pool where they drowned. Of course, in the history of natural disasters, these were not the most tragic in terms of lives lost, but the horror of this loss is jarring.

The 2010 earthquake in Haiti was so devastating it defies description. With 316,000 lives lost, the morgues in Port-au-Prince were overrun with tens of thousands of bodies. Residents were forced to bury the dead in mass graves to stop the spread of disease. In addition, it was reported that 250,000 residential and 30,000 commercial buildings were damaged beyond repair.

The inescapable poverty of Haiti was one of the reasons that there was so much damage; building conditions were so poor that homes and businesses simply couldn't withstand the force of the quake. One rescuer described the early aftermath:

> Everywhere, the acrid smell of bodies hangs in the air. It's just like the stories we are told of the Holocaust—thousands of bodies everywhere. You have to understand that the situation is true madness, and the more time passes, there are more and more bodies, in numbers that cannot be grasped. It is beyond comprehension.[1]

Two years after the quake, an estimated 500,000 people were still without a permanent place of residence.

More recently in Japan, a 9.0 earthquake rocked the ocean floor off the coast of Oshika. The earthquake and resulting tsunami that destroyed the coast killed almost 16,000 people. Again, this level of loss is beyond comprehension.

When you start talking in terms of hundreds of thousands of people killed in a single natural disaster, it is impossible to even grasp the weight of the tragedy. I could go on describing the horror of different natural disasters and the millions of lives affected by them. These natural disasters are sometimes called "acts of God." How can a good and loving God allow these things to happen? How can we cope with these staggering incidents? And how can we help our children understand natural disasters as we sit dumbfounded and overwhelmed, watching the news?

What Went Wrong?

When we try to make sense of such seemingly senseless tragedies, we have to start with what we know about God and then interpret each situation through that knowledge. What do we know about God and the world he created? Is this world as he created it? What do we know about the role we've played in this ongoing devastation?

Man was intended to live in complete harmony with nature. God's original intent was that there would be no natural disasters. Imagine that: a world with perfect weather, with all the animal kingdom as our friends, with ground that yielded wonderful produce that would nourish our perfectly healthy bodies. And then . . . man was tempted through a created being, Satan. He misused the creation, ate from the Tree of the Knowledge of Good and Evil, and with his fall the death and decay of man and of the earth began, too. In Genesis 3 we hear the pronouncement of judgment for Adam's sin. This judgment did not affect only humanity; it also affected the creation as a whole:

> Cursed is the ground because of you; in pain you shall eat of it all the days of your life; thorns and thistles it shall bring forth for you; and you shall eat the plants of the field. By the sweat of your face you shall eat bread, till you return to the ground, for out of it you were taken; for you are dust, and to dust you shall return.
>
> Genesis 3:17–19

In that one moment, the earth that was originally meant to give life and sustain Adam and Eve became a coffin for the dead. Instead of giving life, our planet became a global mortuary, filled with rot, dust, and decay. The very ground that was to produce food for us and partner with us in working to the glory of God was placed under a curse of bondage. The creation itself was to become our adversary and would resist all our efforts to tame and use it; work would be futile. Life would be hard and desperate, and then we would die and return to the earth to await the dissolution of our body. Such is the result of choosing our own way.

Romans 8:19–21 describes creation's pain under the curse:

> For the creation waits with eager longing for the revealing of the sons of God. For the creation was subjected to futility, not willingly, but because of him who subjected it, in hope that the creation itself will be set free from its bondage to corruption and obtain the freedom of the glory of the children of God.

Creation itself is in bondage to corruption. It is not what it once was. "Nature" is not our "mother." If anything, it might be called our older brother who is always kicking sand in our faces. It has become a cruel broker of death and destruction. This is what we see when we watch the devastation of cyclones, tsunamis, earthquakes, volcanoes, and wildfires. But that's not the only place "big brother" makes his presence felt. We see this enmity when weeds choke out our gardens, when oppressive heat kills the elderly, when an E. coli bug lurks in pieces of lettuce served at a restaurant. No, nature is no longer our friend, and it never was our mother. Nature is groaning under the burden of God's curse . . . and it's not happy.

Of course, nature's cursed bondage is obvious from the devastation we see in natural disasters. But this ruin also hits closer to home. As Paul exclaims, "Who will deliver me from this body of death?" (Romans 7:24). In the same way that Paul is crying out for deliverance from the curse brought about by sin, creation also groans for redemption and release. The natural world wants to be delivered from all the decay, the anguish, and the isolation in the animal kingdom. It, too, longs for the days prophesied by Isaiah:

> The wolf shall dwell with the lamb,
>   and the leopard shall lie down with the young goat,

> and the calf and the lion and the fattened calf together;
>> and a little child shall lead them.
> The cow and the bear shall graze;
>> their young shall lie down together;
>> and the lion shall eat straw like the ox.
> The nursing child shall play over the hole of the cobra,
>> and the weaned child shall put his hand on the ad-
>>> der's den.
> They shall not hurt or destroy
>> in all my holy mountain;
> for the earth shall be full of the knowledge of the Lord,
>> as the waters cover the sea.
>>>>> Isaiah 11:6–9

The personification of creation in Romans 8 is what we observe every day, as the effects of our sin are poured out on everything around us. Creation is groaning and waiting "with eager longing for the revealing of the sons of God" (v. 19). Like us, creation is waiting for that last day when Christ, the second Adam, comes back to make everything right again.

What Is Our Hope?

The beauty of the gospel is that it never leaves us with only the bad news. Yes, creation is under a curse. Yes, natural disasters take thousands of lives. But the good news is, there will come a day when Jesus Christ will return and "creation itself will be set free from its bondage to corruption and obtain the freedom of the glory of the children of God" (Romans 8:21). As one Bible commentary put it, "The cosmic fall is not the last word; the last word is with hope."[2]

In his everlasting, compassionate kindness, God offers us hope, even in the decay of the earth. He will not leave everything the way it is. Creation is groaning to give birth, to give new life, to give resurrection from the dead (Romans 8:19). Creation waits as we also await the new life that will be ours. J. B. Phillips paraphrases verse 19 in this way: "The whole creation is on tiptoe to see the wonderful sight of the sons of God coming into their own."[3] Likewise, Eugene Peterson says,

> The created world itself can hardly wait for what's coming next. Everything in creation is being more or less held back. God reins it in until both creation and all the creatures are ready and can be released at the same moment into the glorious times ahead. Meanwhile, the joyful anticipation deepens.[4]

While we endure the tragedy of natural disasters and watch storms and earthquakes tear families apart and ravage landscapes, we can know with complete certainty that this is not the end. There is something bigger, something better, in store for us.

Who Is God? Where Is He? Why Doesn't He Stop This?

There are times when the only hope we can hold on to is the character of our God. We know he never changes. As Psalm 102:27 describes God, "But you are the same, and your years have no end." Just as he worked redemption for Adam and Eve, he will work redemption for the earth and his people. Charles Spurgeon writes, "When we cannot trace God's hand, we must simply trust His heart."[5] This is the truth we hold to in the face of natural disasters. We must simply trust his heart—for "the steadfast love of the Lord is from everlasting to everlasting upon those who fear him" (Psalm 103:17 RSV).

We don't have to fear that God is punishing his children with natural disasters, because all the punishment for all the sins of God's children has already been poured out on the Son at Calvary. However, God may use a natural disaster to bring attention to the fact that life is as fleeting as a breath or vapor:

> You do not know what tomorrow will bring. What is your life? For you are a mist that appears for a little time and then vanishes.

> James 4:14

Under the inspiration of the Holy Spirit, Moses was brought to this same realization:

> The years of our life are seventy, or even by reason of strength eighty; yet their span is but toil and trouble; they are soon gone, and we fly away. Who considers the power of your anger, and your wrath according to the fear of you? So teach us to number our days that we may get a heart of wisdom.

> Psalm 90:10–12

While it is difficult to understand how any good could come from horrific tragedies, we have to look to Scripture and ask for a heart of wisdom. Difficulties—something as paltry as an irritating hangnail all the way to tsunamis—are meant to teach us to look at life circumspectly and to see the true devastation that sin has brought. God's character is not besmirched by the evil we see in the world. In fact, his promise-keeping character that said sin would lead to death ("for in the day that you eat of it you shall surely die"—Genesis 2:17) is upheld. God keeps his promises.

Often people feel that if God was good and powerful, he would prevent the suffering of natural disasters. While it is true that God is both good and powerful (and wise and kind), he never promised he would prevent death, suffering, or catastrophe. On the contrary, he promised that suffering and death would follow disobedience—and it has. We are wise when we

121

realize that all sin has consequences, many unforeseen and long-lasting. Of course, we are not saying that specific disasters are the direct result of specific sins, but rather the entire world is under the curse of sin, and we feel the consequences of that curse in our daily lives, whether we're trying to live for God or not. We are also wise when we learn that life in this world is as Moses described it: "For all our days pass away under your wrath; we bring our years to an end like a sigh" (Psalm 90:9).

God Works Redemptively, Even in Tragedy

Aside from keeping his promise of death for disobedience, is God doing anything else? We have to go back to Romans 8 to see God answering that very question. Right before Saint Paul explains the situation with creation, he encourages us with these hope-building words: "For I consider that the sufferings of this present time are not worth comparing with the glory that is to be revealed to us" (v. 18). Even though there is real suffering caused by the curse that rests on the creation, there is also real hope that one day everything will be made right again. The world is not as it once was, but it is also not as it will be. A day of life, peace, true prosperity, and glory is coming. Pastor Tim Keller puts it this way:

> The biblical view of this is resurrection—not a future that is just a *consolation* for the life we never had but a *restoration* of the life you always wanted. This means that every horrible thing that ever happened will not only be undone and repaired but will in some way make the eventual glory and joy even greater.[6]

We are all waiting for that day. Yes, and even the cursed creation is waiting. Creation longs to be free from the curse and the breach that placed it against us, as our enemy. A day is coming when the entire creation will be scrubbed by fire:

> The heavens and earth that now exist are stored up for fire, being kept until the day of judgment and destruction of the ungodly. . . . But the day of the Lord will come like a thief, and then the heavens will pass away with a roar, and the heavenly bodies will be burned up and dissolved. . . . The heavens will be set on fire and dissolved, and the heavenly bodies will melt as they burn! But according to his promise we are waiting for new heavens and a new earth in which righteousness dwells.
>
> 2 Peter 3:7, 10, 12–13

The Lord is going to do away with this present cursed creation and replace it with something so much more glorious it defies description:

> Then I saw a new heaven and a new earth, for the first heaven and the first earth had passed away, and the sea was no more. And I saw the holy city, new Jerusalem, coming down out of heaven from God, prepared as a bride adorned for her husband. And I heard a loud voice from the throne saying, "Behold, the dwelling place of God is with man. He will dwell with them, and they will be his people, and God himself will be with them as their God. He will wipe away every tear from their eyes, and death shall be no more, neither shall there be mourning, nor crying, nor pain anymore, for the former things have passed away."
>
> Revelation 21:1–4

This, too, is far beyond our understanding, but we accept with faith the goodness that God promises. God will not leave things as they are. He will not allow this futility, suffering, and ultimate death to go on forever. And so we can look forward with hope to his work in this world.

He Is Working for Our Good

Also in Romans 8 are the words that should calm our troubled hearts in any trial:

> And we know that for those who love God all things work together for good, for those who are called according to his purpose. For those whom he foreknew he also predestined to be conformed to the image of his Son, in order that he might be the firstborn among many brothers.
>
> vv. 28–29

The risen Christ is the first example of what is about to happen. He is the first one to be eternally resurrected. He will never experience death again, and one day we will join him. Our hope in the midst of a destructive natural disaster is to remember the end of the story, to remember that Jesus understands the suffering and the groaning, and that he, too, is waiting for all things to be made right again. Our hope is to know that while God does allow natural disasters to take place, he is not ever capricious or heartless. He is keeping his word to us, but he is also restraining the judgment that the whole world deserves. Without his great mercy we might all be faced with natural disasters every day. In his judgment he shows us mercy, and he is also faithful to bless even the wicked with goodness.

> He makes his sun rise on the evil and on the good, and sends rain on the just and on the unjust.
>
> Matthew 5:45

> For he did good by giving you rains from heaven and fruitful seasons, satisfying your hearts with food and gladness.
>
> Acts 14:17

In addition, we can be assured that everything, even our suffering, works together for our good. God is always looking to love us. He is all-powerful and will use every means necessary to love us. He is totally wise and knows the best way to show us his love. God may be doing a work of grace we don't understand. Even though our finite minds do not understand the way that God works or why certain events must take place, we can rest and "trust God's heart." He keeps his promises: He will bring us to new life in a new heaven and new earth where all tears will be dried by his faithful hand.

Talking to Your Kids

Preschool

Praying for families who are affected by natural disaster might be the best way to talk to kids in this age range. They don't possess the ability to completely understand death, let alone the death of children their own age. The numbers of the dead in natural disasters are not something anyone can cognitively process. You can take the time to explain God's character, and then pray with your children for those who have been affected.

Sometimes things happen and we don't understand why. People get hurt and die, and it doesn't seem to make sense. God created the whole world, and he made it perfect. Then Adam and Eve sinned and the world was hurt by their sin. But God has promised that the whole world will one day be made new, and in the meantime we can trust him.

Ages 5 to 10

In this age range, you can start getting a little more detailed about what has been discussed in this chapter. We always want to start with the beginning of the Bible and work our way through the truth about who God is and what he is doing. Truly his character is the only thing that will bring hope in the face of natural disasters.

Sometimes bad things happen and we don't understand why. Moms, dads, and children are hurt or die because of big storms or earthquakes. If we think only about those things and forget about who God is, we will be afraid. But God is the creator of the entire universe. He made the earth we live on, and he made everything around us. In the very beginning when Adam and Eve sinned, part of the punishment for disobeying God was that the earth would change. In the garden of Eden, the earth was perfect, but sin changed that. Now the earth has terrible storms, earthquakes, tsunamis, and other awful things that hurt people. When these things happen, we have to remember what we know about God. He always does what is best for his people. Even though it may not seem like it to us, he is wiser than we are and he has better plans than we do.

Someday God will make everything right again; there will be no death, no sadness, no tears. Nothing happens without a reason. God's love is bigger than all of our sadness, and even when we are sad, he can help us feel better. This doesn't mean we pretend that nothing is sad. It means that even when things are sad, we can remember that God cares for us. We can pray that God would use bad things to make good things happen. This is the way he works. He likes to flip everything around. We don't have to be afraid, because even though we might experience something terrible, God is still bigger, his love is stronger, and he knows the best way to do everything. He promises to always be with us, even in the tough parts of life. All the trouble we see here will one day disappear, and a new heaven and new earth will be made where we will live without any tears.

We must pray that the Holy Spirit makes our children confident in God's character and that he keeps his promises for good. And as terrible as things may seem now, this isn't all there ever will be. This knowledge is the only thing that will carry us when our own reasoning fails us.

Ages 11 and Up

This is the age where children will be able to understand the realities of natural disasters. They will be able to imagine that these things could very well happen to them. Although they may not understand the danger, they are more apt to understand the consequences of an untamed earth.

Many things will happen in your life that you won't understand. When natural disasters occur, all kinds of questions flood into our minds. Why do giant storms kill thousands of people? Why do earthquakes happen? Why is nature so destructive? Can we ever be safe? When there are things in our lives that don't seem to make sense, we have to go back to what we know for certain. We have to remember who God is and what he says about himself in the Bible. Our minds won't ever completely understand the way God works because he is God and we aren't.

God created the world perfectly. When Adam and Eve sinned, part of the punishment for their sin was that the earth would be affected. It would change from being a place of life and peace to being a place of death and destruction. The Bible says the earth is hurting and waiting for God to come back and make everything right again. The good news is that God will come back and make everything right again. God is love (1 John 4:8), so even if we don't understand why certain things happen, we can remember that he does love us even when it looks like he doesn't. God is also wise, so when a disaster doesn't make sense to us, we can know that he is working everything out for our good and to make himself look more amazing. He is also teaching us not to think that we are invincible.

God is all-powerful, so we don't need to feel afraid. Even when nature looks out of control, God is using every single thing that happens in each of our lives to do good. Nothing that happens is wasted or out of his control. This is hard to understand when we see lots of people die or get hurt, but we must pray for faith to believe what he says about himself. One day all sadness and death will be gone, and we won't have to fear nature any longer. Until that day, we can trust that God will be with us, that he loves us, and that nothing happens that he can't use for our good.

In a Nutshell

- Natural disasters are actually "unnatural," because they were not to be part of the world that God created in the beginning.
- The entire creation has been harmed by the curse mankind brought upon itself through sin.
- At the end of time, Jesus will return and make a new heaven and a new earth where there won't be any natural disasters.
- In the meantime, we can trust that God will use all the suffering in this world for his own good purposes.

9

Why Do People Fight and Kill?

I remember those first few days after September 11, 2001. My oldest son, Wesley, was only three at the time. Like everyone else, my husband and I were hungry for information. Like you, we wanted to know what had happened, if anyone had been found alive in the rubble that was once the Twin Towers, and who was to blame for this terrifying carnage. We were glued to the television. We watched President George W. Bush stand atop that wreckage at Ground Zero, and we wept and prayed.

We tried to make sense of a senseless tragedy. And there was our little Wesley and his little brother, Hayden, still in diapers, looking at us with questioning eyes, seeing those images, and asking, "Mommy, Daddy, why?"

Yes, why? We knew then, perhaps as we had never known before, that part of our job was to try to explain what we were seeing. At the same time, we sought to protect those little eyes from seeing things they weren't ready for. The truth was, we didn't think we were ready to see it, either, and we sure didn't feel like we had any satisfying answers.

War Is Nothing New

Human history has been forged in a cauldron of sickening violence. From the first murder in Genesis 4 down through the centuries to the greatest act of violence in the slaying of the innocent One on Calvary, and in every century since, mankind has proven that viciousness is second nature to him. What century hasn't been stained with blood?

Violence takes many forms. It occurs in homes. It occurs nationally, when one country takes up arms against another. And it strikes smaller groups of citizens, when terrorists attack non-combatants without national fiat.

Again, this is nothing new. The Bible is a book of profound honesty, so its pages, too, are filled with stories of hideous brutality. Because it portrays us as we truly are, though, it is the only narrative that can actually give us hope. As the editors of the *Dictionary of Biblical Imagery* note,

> The Bible is not a "nice" book that hides the sordid side of life. The Bible is a book of thoroughgoing realism. The Bible's stories of violence demonstrate the depths of depravity to which the human race descends. Paradoxically, though, the nadir of depravity represented by biblical stories of violence is also the climax of the Bible's story of redemption. The violence of the cross is the pivot point of redemption.[1]

We can trust that if the Lord was able to redeem even the most horrific act of violence—the crucifixion—he will be able to turn the violence we face for good. God has made it clear that he does not approve of sinful violence. In fact, he says he hates it:

> There are six things that the Lord hates,
> seven that are an abomination to him:
> haughty eyes, a lying tongue,
> and hands that shed innocent blood,
> a heart that devises wicked plans,
> feet that make haste to run to evil.
>
> Proverbs 6:16–18

And yet, in his own wisdom and for his own glory, God allows things he hates to continue in our world. We do not know why he allows atrocities, but we do know that he is good, wise, loving, and powerful. And we know that this world of violence will not continue unabated forever.

The Violence Within

Violence is inescapable. In our family's neighborhood, we recently witnessed a SWAT team action; my ten-year-old daughter informed me that the neighbor had severely beaten the woman he was living with. Even children who are protected in their homes from the abuse of evil outsiders frequently experience violence—from their siblings, from bullies at school, and even at church when a friend does something to hurt them.

Violence is part of the human condition. It is part of our brokenness, and it is not necessarily a result of living in a violent environment. The first murder to ever occur was Cain's slaying of Abel. Cain had never seen anyone kill another person—he didn't learn violence from his environment. Rather, it was already in his heart.

> Cain rose up against his brother Abel and killed him. Then the Lord said to Cain, "Where is Abel your brother?" He said, "I do not know; am I my brother's keeper?" And the Lord said,

"What have you done? The voice of your brother's blood is crying to me from the ground. And now you are cursed from the ground, which has opened its mouth to receive your brother's blood from your hand."

Genesis 4:8–11

How did the Lord, who knows the hearts of all men (1 Chronicles 28:9), diagnose the motive behind Cain's action? In Genesis 4, Cain was very angry because Abel's sacrifice had been accepted by God and his had not. In kindness the Lord warned him,

Why are you angry, and why has your face fallen? If you do well, will you not be accepted? And if you do not do well, sin is crouching at the door. Its desire is for you, but you must rule over it.

Genesis 4:6–7

Just like the rest of us, Cain's problem was that he was a sinner. Cain was angry and killed his brother because he was envious of him. He was envious because he wanted something from God he thought he deserved and hadn't received. Jesus tells us where his envy came from:

What comes out of a person is what defiles him. For from within, out of the heart of man, come evil thoughts . . . murder . . . coveting . . . envy. . . . All these evil things come from within, and they defile a person.

Mark 7:20–23

Thankfully, even in the midst of this heartbreaking scene of fratricide, we catch a glimpse of the redemption that is to come. Another's blood would also be spilled out of enraged envy (Mark 15:10). And this One's blood would cry out to God from the ground, too, but his blood would cry out for our forgiveness rather than judgment.

Why Do We Fight?

> What causes quarrels and what causes fights among you? Is it
> not this, that your passions are at war within you? You desire
> and do not have, so you murder. You covet and cannot obtain,
> so you fight and quarrel.

> James 4:1–2

Whenever you witness violence—whether in your own heart,
your own home, or on TV—this passage from James tells you
where to look as you try to answer the "why?" question: "Why
do people fight and quarrel?" People have such a desire for something that they are willing to harm others to get it. We see
something we think we need to be happy and we're willing to
kill to obtain it. Cain wanted the approval Abel had, and since
he couldn't kill God, who was withholding that approval from
him, he decided to kill his brother (who was loved by God and
made in his image). At heart, our willingness to harm others
flows out of an idolatrous desire for something we love more
than God. We covet what others have. We think God is wrong
in withholding it from us, and since we can't kill him, we kill
those who have thwarted our acquisition of the overly valued
object, whatever it might be.

What might some of those desires be in our own hearts?
Our desire to be first, to be well thought of, to be loved and
respected, to have fun, to have what others have, to be comfortable and secure; these are all motives that would drive us
to harm others. We are an idolatrous people and are willing
to fight, quarrel, and even kill for what we think will make
us happy. And when jealousy rules us, it will always end in
hatred and sin. Only God's jealousy is pure enough to end
in love.

Violence in the Home

Whenever a sinner lives with another sinner, violence should be expected. Spouses harm each other, parents abuse their children, children hurt their siblings. Almost 10 percent of children reported seeing a family assault during one year, a national survey reported. And 1.5 million incidents of family violence were reported to a federal bureau between 1996 and 2001.[2]

Family members hurt each other because they are not getting what they think they need to be happy. When a father thinks he has to have respect from his son in order to be happy, he is on the pathway to violence against him. Whenever a mom thinks she cannot stand one more "No!" in response to her requests, she's liable to lash out in anger. There are fights because a brother steals another brother's toy and the offended brother believes justice must be served. In every scenario and thousands of others like them, people feel like it is their right to make others experience their wrath and pay for their sins against them.

We are all bent in on ourselves; we all believe we are responsible for making ourselves happy and that others should be given judgment rather than mercy. When we make personal happiness and fulfillment our ultimate functional god or ruling idol, we will surely find sin crouching at the door.

Christ Jesus was the only human in history who laid down every single desire on the altar of love for his Father. He was the only One willing to trust his Father and patiently await the fulfillment of all he longed for. He was the only One who didn't use violence to intimidate, and yet he was the One who was violently beaten for us.

> Like a lamb that is led to the slaughter, and like a sheep that before its shearers is silent, so he opened not his mouth.
>
> Isaiah 53:7

> When he was reviled, he did not revile in return; when he suffered, he did not threaten, but continued entrusting himself to him who judges justly.
>
> 1 Peter 2:23

The only truly innocent victim in all of history is our sweet Savior.

War

Although North America is in the middle of a war right now, unless we're involved in the military, most of us go about our days almost completely unaware of it. That's because warfare has changed so drastically in the last one hundred years. Nowadays, one force can attack another without even being on the same continent. To many of our children, the pictures of devastation caused by war get tangled up in images of video games and movies. But the violence of war is real, and the lives that are taken are those of real fathers and mothers, sons and daughters.

Yes, war is costly and terrible, but not all war is evil. There are times when war is necessary. For instance, when one nation attacks another nation because they want something the other nation has, most Christians would say it is not sinful to respond in self-defense. When Imperial Japan bombed Pearl Harbor on December 7, 1941, it was right for the United States to react. When Germany attacked our allies in Europe, we had an obligation as members of an alliance to help defend them. Sometimes the response to an attack causes great devastation, but when a war is entered into with the aim to protect lives, it is good.

The Bible is clear about war being necessary in certain cases. Man is evil, and at times evil men become too powerful. The

135

only way these evil men can be stopped is by one nation declaring war on another nation. Psalm 82:3–4 puts it this way: "Give justice to the weak and the fatherless; maintain the right of the afflicted and the destitute. Rescue the weak and the needy; deliver them from the hand of the wicked."

Of course, there are also times when war should not be used to accomplish what we think might be good or necessary. For instance, war should never be used to "Christianize" a nation or a people. Jesus showed us this in John 18:36:

> Jesus answered, "My kingdom is not of this world. If my kingdom were of this world, my servants would have been fighting, that I might not be delivered over to the Jews. But my kingdom is not from the world."

Ultimately, we know that God is the One in charge, and his sovereignty is intact even when things seem out of control. Wars don't take God by surprise. In fact, Jesus actually promised us there would be wars until his return. While wars and rumors of wars are disheartening to us, he is sovereign over every circumstance, and we can rest in his strong arms.

> And you will hear of wars and rumors of wars. See that you are not alarmed, for this must take place, but the end is not yet. For nation will rise against nation, and kingdom against kingdom, and there will be famines and earthquakes in various places. All these are but the beginning of the birth pains.
>
> Matthew 24:6–8

Our God knows and sees how alarmed we may become in the face of war, so Jesus spoke these words of comfort to us. English pastor Charles Spurgeon said, "Fate is blind; providence has eyes." Wars do not happen by chance. The Lord knows and sees, and he also cares deeply about his people, for,

"Precious in the sight of the Lord is the death of his saints" (Psalm 116:15).

Terrorism

The most sinister form of war is terrorism. Terrorism happens when a group of individuals seeks to use violence and intimidation in the pursuit of their political aims without a national authorization. Like other forms of violence, the terrorist is fighting for what he thinks will ultimately make him happy. Differing from other forms of war, the terrorist is willing to kill not only enemy combatants, but also unsuspecting civilians. The terrorist thrives on creating terror. He preys upon our fear of the unknown and our inability to protect ourselves from attack. It is in that way that he perpetuates fear, panic, and terror.

As Christians, we don't have to fear the future. We have a hope that is stronger than the terrorist's ability to produce fear. Jesus teaches us,

> And do not fear those who kill the body but cannot kill the soul. Rather fear him who can destroy both soul and body in hell. Are not two sparrows sold for a penny? And not one of them will fall to the ground apart from your Father. But even the hairs of your head are all numbered. Fear not, therefore; you are of more value than many sparrows.
>
> Matthew 10:28–31

We have a heavenly Father whose name is El Roi, which means, "a God who sees" (Genesis 16:13). Although an untimely death is certainly terrible, Jesus teaches us that dying isn't the worst thing that can happen to us; dying apart from Christ is. If you are in him, you don't need to fear death.

Talking to Our Kids

Preschool

Of course, you won't want to frighten children unnecessarily, so perhaps it would be best to let preschoolers lead in this area. Answer the questions they ask, but remember to keep it simple and concrete. Obviously, it is also wise to minimize their exposure to graphic images of destruction as much as you can.

> There are very bad people in the world. There are people who want things so badly they will do anything to get those things. Have you ever wanted a toy so badly that you hit someone to get it? You know that anger you feel? Some very bad people feel that anger all the time and they want to hurt people. We don't have to be afraid, though, because God is stronger than the strongest person in the whole world. God uses people in the army and the police to protect us from those bad people.
>
> When you are scared of someone, you should always talk to us. We can help you if someone is hurting you. God put us in your life to help keep you safe. We can pray for the people who are so angry that they hurt others. God can change anyone's heart. His love is stronger than their hate.

You don't need to go into detail about the horrors of war. Just assure children that God is in control and you will do your best to take care of them.

Ages 5 to 10

Children in this age group will hear and understand more about violence. They have certainly experienced violence at this point in their lives. They have also probably heard about 9/11 at school or on the news. Again, we want to try to reassure them that even though we don't know the future, we know our God.

138

There are bad people in the world. Each one of us has a desire in our hearts to get what we want when we want it. Do you ever feel so angry that you want to hit someone because they do something you don't like? Well, some bad people who hurt others feel that anger all the time. In fact, they are controlled by their anger. When you are controlled by anger, you do all sorts of terrible things, and you think that what you are doing is right or you think the person you are being mean to deserves it. That is how our enemies or terrorists think. They are so convinced they are right that they don't care about anybody else.

I know this might sound scary. We don't have to be afraid, though, because Jesus promised that he would always take care of us. God put us, Mom and Dad, into your life to help protect you. God has also given us the military and the police to protect us. If anybody ever does anything to hurt you or threatens to hurt you, you need to make sure you tell us. People who are controlled by anger need someone stronger to stop them from hurting others. We can pray for people who are hurting others. Jesus prayed for the people who were killing him. Even though their hate is strong, God's unstoppable love can change them. His love is stronger than the deepest hate.

Reassure your children that God knows the future and nothing can happen to them that won't end up being for their good and his glory. We don't always understand how God works, but we can know that he works in ways too glorious for us to know.

Ages 11 and Up

Children in this age range have probably seen videos from 9/11 or other terrible scenes: school shootings, the Boston Marathon bombing, etc. These kids have a real understanding of what terrorism is. We can be frank with them about the harshness of war, but we always want to do so in the context of giving hope in our strong God.

People have been hurting each other from the very beginning of time. You have heard the story about how Cain killed Abel because he was jealous of him. You know about terrorist attacks that have happened since then. You know how evil people can be. What you also need to understand is that the anger that drives those evil people is also in your own heart.

Have you ever felt so angry at people you wanted to hurt them? That anger is how violent people feel all the time. The Bible tells us we don't need to be afraid of people who can kill us. That might sound a little funny, but let me explain. We don't need to fear someone who wants to kill us because, if you are a believer, death is not your final destination. Death just brings you to Jesus. On the other hand, we do need to be afraid of God, who sees into our hearts and sees all our anger, and will judge all of humanity for its sin. If you think your own goodness or kindness is going to make God love you, you are wrong. Only the goodness of Jesus Christ will be enough to keep us from God's judgment.

Sometimes when people act in violence, we want to hide. And while it is right to try to get out of the path of a violent person, we have a wonderful place to hide. We can hide in Christ. He lived perfectly. He never was sinfully angry at anyone, and he was never violent with anyone. If we believe God is as good as he says he is, and if we believe we are sinners who need to be forgiven, then when God looks at us, all he sees is the perfect life of Christ. We are hidden in him. We don't need to be afraid of what violent people can do to us. We can pray that God changes the hearts of those who love violence. Their hatred may seem strong, but God's love is stronger. He can change the heart of any person.

All children know what it is like to feel threatened and afraid of being harmed. Whether that harm comes to them from parents, siblings, friends, or foreign enemies, they need to be taught to trust in God. You can remind them of these words from the Psalms: "When I am afraid, I put my trust in you. In God, whose word I praise, in God I trust; I shall not be afraid. What can flesh do to me?" (Psalm 56:3–4).

In a Nutshell

- Conflict and violence have been part of the human experience since Cain murdered his brother Abel.
- The seeds of violence and war are in the hearts of all people who want something they do not have and are willing to fight to get it.
- Not all violence is bad. Sometimes people have to use violence to protect themselves from other angry, greedy people.
- We do not have to be afraid, because for the Christian, even death cannot separate us from the love of Christ.

10

The Good News
That Should Always Be Shared

A h . . . good news. Don't you need some good news today?
I know I do. We all long for a message that will give us
hope—hope that there is more to life than these terrible realities
we've been talking about. We all need to know that there are
satisfying answers and, more important, that a real Someone
knows the answers and loves us, too. We need to know there is
a plan, a reason, an overarching purpose for all the brokenness,
grief, and suffering we see.

It's easy to think that the questions and challenges our families face are greater than the challenges from Bible times. Perhaps
you wish your family was living in a less complicated, more
innocent world. But life in the ancient Near East was brutal,
filled with superstition, poverty, plagues, cruelty, and early death.
There was oppression and slavery and continual wars. Yet parents and their children were able to find (and rejoice in!) the good
news even in the midst of that darkness. They were desperate

for good news, and they found it in the message of the gospel. It's the best news anyone has ever heard, and it speaks to us just as it did to them.

We are not alone. God is here. He is holy and he is loving. In fact, he's so loving he was willing to sacrifice what he loved most in order to bring us to himself. No matter what we see around us, there is one overriding message, one blessed truth:

> For God so loved the world, that he gave his only Son, that whoever believes in him should not perish but have eternal life. For God did not send his Son into the world to condemn the world, but in order that the world might be saved through him.
>
> John 3:16–17

Here's the good news: God loves us and was willing to pay the price his love and holiness demanded. But he hasn't just loved us disinterestedly from afar; instead, he has adopted us as dearly loved members of his family.

> See what kind of love the Father has given to us, that we should be called children of God; and so we are. . . . Beloved, we are God's children now, and what we will be has not yet appeared; but we know that when he appears we shall be like him, because we shall see him as he is.
>
> 1 John 3:1–2

Of course, to do this, he had to overcome the problem of our rebellion, alienation, and sin. In his wisdom and great love, he solved our unsolvable problem by sending his Son to live perfectly and then die shamefully by our hand and in our place. And then, glorious good news, on that first Easter Sunday morning, the Father raised his Son to life again, declaring that our gravest problems—our sin, and the resultant curse of death and alienation from God—had been solved. Listen, if God can solve this problem, we don't need to be concerned about whether he'll be able to make right everything that troubles us now. Isn't that good news?

More Good News: You Don't Have to Be the Bible-Answer Mom or Dad

The ability of your children to believe and understand the answers you give to them—even your ability to explain these answers to them—is not what will save your children. Understanding spiritual truth and a faith from understanding that truth is a matter of the work of the Spirit:

> The natural person does not accept the things of the Spirit of God, for they are folly to him, and he is not able to understand them because they are spiritually discerned.
>
> 1 Corinthians 2:14

> For by grace you have been saved through faith. And this is not your own doing; it is the gift of God, not a result of works, so that no one may boast.
>
> Ephesians 2:8–9

> But to all who did receive him [Jesus], who believed in his name, he gave the right to become children of God, who were born, *not of blood nor of the will of the flesh nor of the will of man, but of God.*
>
> John 1:12–13

It takes the Holy Spirit to enable children and their parents to first understand and then believe the good news. But the good news is that the Holy Spirit continues to work even in our day; in fact, he may be working in your child's heart right at this moment as you read this.

Of course, that's not to say we shouldn't try to answer our children's questions. For we have been commanded to "bring them up in the discipline and instruction of the Lord" (Ephesians 6:4). God commands us to be faithful parents because God uses means to bring faith and salvation. He may use your faithful words, flawlessly articulated. Or he may use your stumbling, halting, hesitating words and your doubt. We don't know what he will use; but we do know that if he could use an uneducated coward like Peter or an overly educated murderer like Paul, he certainly can use any of us.

Let's be honest: There will be times when your children will come to you with difficult questions and you just won't have it in you to answer them. God isn't looking for a superstar of a parent in order to save your kids; he is looking for you to trust him with their salvation. He knows your weaknesses; he remembers that you are dust. And then he uses your weakness to make himself look great.

There is an old parable that illustrates this truth: *Whenever you see a turtle sitting atop a fence post, you can know he didn't get there by himself.* And that, I think, is the point demonstrated when we see God using imperfect parents and their flawed words as means to bring children to faith. Whenever we remember to say something gospel-oriented to our kids or are able to remind them of Jesus in a difficult situation, we can be assured that it is because of God's grace. He has taken the turtle and has placed it up on that fence post to prove that this success wasn't the turtle's doing. Sure, it is important to be informed, but God uses the foolish things of this world to shame the wise. We can be free from thinking that our children's understanding or salvation rests on our wisdom or strength. He delights in taking nothings and bringing something wonderful out of them to glorify himself.

But God chose what is foolish in the world to shame the wise; God chose what is weak in the world to shame the strong; God chose what is low and despised in the world, even things that are not, to bring to nothing things that are, so that no human being might boast in the presence of God.

1 Corinthians 1:27–29

God's use of short-legged, slow turtles shames those who think they are smart and strong and oh, so in control. And he just loves to do it.

Even More Good News: God Patiently Bears With Our Weaknesses

Being a parent is hard, and being a parent who wants to raise your children to love God is even harder. It's so hard to know when to discipline, how to discipline, and why we should discipline. The pressure of "getting it right" is enough to make me want to give up in utter confusion. And then, when you throw in all of the difficult topics covered in this book, almost every one of us will feel terribly ill-equipped. The books, the blogs, the conversations at the park that revolve around these questions are endless. We want to be sure we are doing the right job, being the right parent, so we can raise the right kids . . . and still we remain weak little turtles just like them.

As you've considered how God uses turtles to accomplish his goals, remember that your children are your children . . . they, too, are weak little turtles. Not only are they weak because they are flawed human beings, they are weak because they are immature. They don't have the intellectual faculties to understand everything you might be saying. With all the emphasis on helping our children mature, I think we may have forgotten that we are raising children. We have forgotten that they are actually just kids. They think like kids, speak like kids, reason like kids. They don't have decades of experience under their belts like you and me. Paul himself spoke of his own immaturity:

> When I was a child, I spoke like a child, I thought like a child, I reasoned like a child. When I became a man, I gave up childish ways.
>
> 1 Corinthians 13:11

When Paul was a child he didn't think in adult ways, and his immaturity wasn't sin. He was a child, so he spoke, thought, and reasoned like a child. This is good news for children and their parents. We don't have to expect our children to act or reason as though they are adults. By God's grace (and far too soon) our children will give up their "childish ways." But for now we must remember that they are still weak, inexperienced, and immature.

So often we expect our children to think and be able to understand as we do. For instance, we expect them to know that when they swing a rope in a certain way, it will probably hit someone in the face. We expect them to think through the fact that when they sit on the dog—which is such great fun, and the closest thing to the horse they want but you won't buy—the dog might bite them or might get hurt. We expect them to think like an adult, but they aren't adults; they are children.

The tragic thing is, in our desire to raise godly children, we sometimes punish childishness as though it were sin. We forget that they have only been alive for, say, eight years, and only have eight years of knowledge. We accuse them of being unloving, or unkind, or foolish as though they actually thought through what they were about to do and decided that jumping off the highest branch and landing next to or on their sister was the best course of action. Talk about exasperating! When I am next to a techie and do something stupid on my computer and hear the inevitable sigh of displeasure, I feel like an idiot. "No, I actually didn't know that if I hit that button, my entire computer would blow up." I'm a turtle, too. My ability to know all I should know and project probable consequences is not what it should be, either.

Now, please don't misunderstand. I am not saying we should excuse sin. When we see sin, we must talk about forgiveness and a Savior. I am all for disciplining children when they sin. But I would love to ask the question—and have you ask yourself: *Is this truly sin, or is this child just thinking like a child?* We can take those opportunities of childlike thinking and use them to gently, patiently explain what all our years of living have taught us. As I write that, I laugh; there is so much more I need to learn, too. I am sure my parents would agree.

The Gospel and the Holy Spirit

I often get asked if my kids get sick of me talking about grace and about Jesus. The answer is, "Of course!" In my own life I, too, tire of hearing the message of the gospel. That isn't because the message of the gospel isn't true or there is something lacking in it. My boredom and apathy with the gospel is just a testament to the hardness of my heart. I need the work of the Holy Spirit to make the words of Christ alive to me, too. So it is with our children. We can share the gospel, but the Holy Spirit must do his work. In moments when you have no idea what to say, whisper a prayer for help, confessing your neediness. Do you need wisdom? Ask the Lord for it.

> If you call out for insight and raise your voice for understanding,
> if you seek it like silver and search for it as for hidden treasures,

149

then you will understand the fear of the Lord and find the knowledge of God. For the Lord gives wisdom.

Proverbs 2:3–6

If any of you lacks wisdom, let him ask God, who gives generously to all without reproach, and it will be given him.

James 1:5

You can ask the Holy Spirit to help you remember and see again how beautiful Christ is. Ask him to do his work in your heart. I have been delightfully amazed how the good news speaks in every circumstance. We have the sweetest Savior who sympathizes with us in every situation.

Did You See Him?

It is my hope that you saw the scarlet thread of redemption running through every answer in this book. This scarlet thread is the story that we base our hope on—it is the story of Christ's pure life given in payment for ours, the story of his redeeming blood shed as the "Lamb of God, who takes away the sin of the world" (John 1:29).

- Man was created in the image of God.
- Man chose to be his own god, to make his own way, and to try to be his own savior.
- This decision to sin had deep and universal consequences in the life of every person and even in the created universe.
- But God in his steadfast love and ever-renewed mercy made a way to bring man back home. For before the worlds were even created, God the Father, God the Son, and God the Spirit wrote the love story for the ages.
- A new man, a second Adam, would be tested in thirty-three years of suffering and would pass the test. He would obey

150

every moment of every day so that all the obedience we lack would be supplied.

- Then that new man, our Brother, our obedient Representative, would die the death we deserve.
- And then God would declare his satisfaction with all that his Son did by raising him from the tomb on the third day.
- This good news about what God has done for us is the news that we need to share all the time. It means we are not only forgiven of our sins, but also are counted perfectly obedient.

Man would reject, God would pursue. Man would hate, God would love. Man would mar, God would redeem. Man would sin, God would forgive. This is the story—the answer—we tell our children. This is the beauty that captivates hearts and minds. We don't need to tell them a story about being better or doing more. We don't need to tell them a story about an angry God who is waiting to gleefully punish them for their sins. We tell them about a God who sees, who loves, and who is all-powerful. We tell them the story of a God who doesn't ignore pain, but rather sent his Son to embrace it. We tell them the story of a God who doesn't waste pain, but rather subjects all things to his glorious will. And we tell them the story about a God who doesn't ask us to pretend that life doesn't hurt, but rather asks us to bring all our hurt to him.

He is the God who understands hurt; Jesus was a man of sorrows and acquainted with grief (Isaiah 53:3). Jesus was despised and rejected by those he loved. He felt our shame, knew our pain, relates with our sorrow. He himself is the good news! He was crushed for our iniquities and pierced for our transgressions. He is our Savior. The One who was oppressed and afflicted comes to us and strengthens us under each difficult question we face. This is the Jesus we share with our children.

This is the One we point them to when they are afraid or hurting or confused.

You see, brothers and sisters, God never calls on us to keep it all together so that our children will be saved. He does call on us to rest in faith in his tender arms. We can leave our children there, too. We can feel the real pain of sin, of death, of confusion, and we can bring it all to him. He doesn't despise us for our weakness; it is the very thing that draws him to us. Embracing our weakness, embracing our inability to understand all of life's questions, will pull us toward him. Let your children know there is only one good story—only one satisfying answer. There is meaning and hope behind every hurt and disappointment. And if they are God's children, their redemption is the most sure truth in the universe.

He Is the God Who Sees

Through every question, through every trial, we serve El Roi, the God who sees, the God who "looks after me" (Genesis 16:13). He looks after us, and he looks after our children. He doesn't punish us capriciously or subject us to frivolous pain. He sees the best way for each of us to know him, and then he leads us down that path. Your kids don't need you to be strong and totally capable; they need to see that you are, like them, dependent and weak, but that you have a strong and capable God. Build confidence in him. Pray for guidance and understanding as you seek to answer your kids' questions. And then rest in the truth that he can and does use every situation to bring himself glory.

How do you share the gospel with your children? You soak your own soul in it daily. As you remember that you are loved by him, you can give that same grace to your children. Grace upon grace is yours, and grace upon grace is your children's, too. Giving them the good news can be as simple as telling them that they are sinners in need of a Rescuer.

Your children see sin, pain, and hurt every day. Younger children may not understand all of the theological implications behind their friend stealing a toy from them, but they do understand the pain. Children might be confused as to why people act so unkindly, but we can use their pain as an opportunity to talk with them about the universality of sin. Each one of us experiences pain because of sin. Every one of us needs help. Rather than telling our children they need to become better people, we can give them good news: Help has to come from outside of them, and the Helper has come!

Every day our children hear messages of bad news, and they are told that all the answers they need are inside of themselves, or told to believe or trust in themselves. Why? Because our children are sinners, and neither we, nor they, are trustworthy. This bad news is a poison advertised as a cure. Anti-gospel messages tell children to trust in their own goodness and faithfulness. But at the end of the day, how much goodness or faithfulness does any one of us actually have? This is simply bad news. We all need a drink from outside our own hearts. We need the living water Christ offered:

> If anyone thirsts, let him come to me and drink. Whoever believes in me, as the Scripture has said, "Out of his heart will flow rivers of living water."
>
> John 7:37–38

God Sympathizes With Us

The living water is a message of Christ's perfect life, substitutionary death, and bodily resurrection, in our place.

So when your children don't see how the gospel intersects with everyday life, pray. Pray that the Holy Spirit will show you the reality of Hebrews 4:14–16:

> Since then we have a great high priest who has passed through the heavens, Jesus, the Son of God, let us hold fast our confession. For we do not have a high priest who is unable to sympathize with our weaknesses, but one who in every respect has been tempted as we are, yet without sin. Let us then with confidence draw near to the throne of grace, that we may receive mercy and find grace to help in time of need.

God sympathizes with us. He feels our pain, understands and knows us. This is the answer we can give our children when we, like them, are filled with questions, confusion, and doubt. Nineteenth-century pastor Octavius Winslow wrote of this passage in Hebrews:

> He is not a High Priest who can be indifferent to your present assault, since he was pierced by Satan, and in a measure is still pierced by the fiery darts which now pierce you. Accept your present temptation as sent to make you better acquainted with His preciousness, His sympathy, His grace, His changeless love.[1]

Pastor John Piper preached about these verses, too:

> Jesus can sympathize with us in our pain and our dying, because he experienced excruciating pain and entered all the way into death. And he can sympathize with us in our allurements to sin, because he was tempted—
> To lie (to save his life)
> And to steal (to help his poor mother when his father died)
> And to covet (all the nice things Zacchaeus owned)
> And to dishonor his parents (when they were more strict than others)

And to take revenge (when he was wrongly accused)

And to lust (when Mary wiped his feet with her hair)

And to pout with self-pity (when his disciples fell asleep in his last hour of trial)

And to murmur at God (when John the Baptist died at the whim of a dancing girl)

And to gloat over his accusers (when they couldn't answer his questions)

Jesus knows the battle. He fought it all the way to the end. And he defeated the monster every time. So he was tested like we are and the Bible says he is a sympathetic High Priest. He does not roll his eyes at your pain or cluck his tongue at your struggle with sin.[2]

Jesus was touched with our feelings, and he is still touched with what we feel. Every circumstance that you and your family go through is understood *by experience* by him. He has good news for you in every circumstance. Pray that you will be able to see and believe the truth about what he has done and that you'll be able to give it to your children, too.

Don't let confusion or feelings of inadequacy keep you from trying to share the gospel. The Holy Spirit is stronger than all your inadequacies. He is stronger than your foolishness. There is good news for average parents. Reading books and learning the correct way to explain things is a good thing, but never put your confidence in your knowledge. Rather, "Trust in the Lord with all your heart, and do not lean on your own understanding" (Proverbs 3:5).

There is a place of rest for you. You can trust his heart. You can trust in his love for you.

So go ahead. Strive to tell your kids the good news. Pray about it whenever it comes into your heart. A simple "Lord, help me know how to speak" will suffice. Pray that God would give you an opportunity with your children. Pray that he would give you words. Pray that your children's hearts would be receptive. But then after all of that, rest. Rest in who he is, rest in God's unchangeable character, rest in his steadfast love, rest in his overwhelming goodness to you.

The Good News for Kids

Preschool

This age is prime for sharing the gospel. You don't have to use big words or long speeches. It is as simple as pointing out the sin your children have done, and then telling them they need a Savior. For instance, if your child hits another child, you can tell her:

God asks us to always be kind and to love others. You just hit your friend, and that wasn't kind or loving. You need Someone to help you live the way God asks us to live. Jesus lived the way God asks us to live. He never hit anybody. Jesus also took all the punishment for every time you and I are unkind to someone. Jesus is your Rescuer. Jesus is your help.

This little speech may be too much for some preschoolers and not enough for others. The main ideas they need to come away with are that they sin and God forgives. Emphasize that God only forgives those who believe that he is good and that he loves them, even though they are sinners.

Ages 5 to 10

In this age group, your child will have a little more ability to pay attention and understand. Again, you should know your child, know what she can handle. You don't want to overload children with theological words, but you can also expect most children to be able to listen to you talk for a few minutes. Typically most kids can sit for hours in front of a movie, so a couple of minutes with you shouldn't be too difficult for them. Let's stick with the example of your child hurting another child, either verbally or physically:

> God has given us two rules: one is to love him more than anything else, and the other is to love those around us. When you say unkind things to others, you are breaking both of those rules. God has promised to punish all sin because God is good and hates sin. So when we do wrong, God owes us a punishment. But Jesus came and always obeyed every rule. He always loved God and he always loved everyone around him. But Jesus died on the cross, taking our place and getting the punishment God owed us. He took the punishment you deserve.
>
> If you believe what God says about you and what he has said about what Jesus has done for you, then in God's eyes it will be as though you have been punished when really it was Jesus being punished for you. And all the good things Jesus did—loving God and loving others—in God's eyes it will be as though you were that obedient and loving. When you feel like you want to hurt someone, you can remember that Jesus is praying for you, too. He loves you even while you are angry. The only thing that will stop you from hurting other people is to remember how Jesus loves you. Even when you disobey and do hurt others, Jesus still loves you. He always loves us. His love should make us love others.

Ages 11 and Up

Children this age will be able to begin to understand the more difficult concepts of the Bible. Soaking your own soul in the gospel will in turn help you talk to your children. In the section that follows, we have suggested several books to explain even more the gospel of grace.

You have broken the rules God has given you in the Bible. The rules are that we must love God above all others, and that we must love our neighbor the way we love ourselves. God tells us that when we break the rules, we sin against him and need to pay for our sins.

He has asked us to live perfectly, and when we don't, he says we have to pay for our sins. He knows we can't do it by ourselves. Because he knows us and loves us, he sent Jesus to live and love perfectly and then die in our place for us. Jesus is God's Son and actually is God himself. He came to earth and lived the life we couldn't live. He obeyed every single rule in the Bible every single second of his entire life. Then Jesus died for our sins. He took all the punishment for every sin you have committed, every sin you are committing, and every sin you will commit in the future. When God looks at you, he doesn't count your sin against you anymore. You are forgiven and made right before him. All he asks you to do is believe that you are as sinful as he says you are, and that he is as good as he says he is.

God doesn't only love you when you are good. God loves you all the time. He is that kind. As you remember these thoughts of God's goodness to you in Jesus Christ, you will be able to be kind to others, even when you don't feel like it. And you can know that when you are deciding how to live, Jesus is praying for you. He knows how it feels to want to hurt others, he understands the pain of being hurt. The crazy good news, though, is even when you don't remember or you choose to be unkind, when you do remember, he is still loving you and running after you.

In a Nutshell

- We are more sinful and flawed than we ever dared believe. We are more loved and welcomed than we ever dared hope.
- Jesus Christ sympathizes with us.
- It is the Holy Spirit's job to change hearts.

Recommended Resources for Further Study

Parenting

Give Them Grace: Dazzling Your Kids with the Love of Jesus by Elyse Fitzpatrick and Jessica Thompson (Crossway)

When Good Kids Make Bad Choices by Dr. Jim Newheiser, Elyse Fitzpatrick, and Dr. Laura Hendrickson (Harvest House)

You Never Stop Being a Parent by Dr. Jim Newheiser and Elyse Fitzpatrick (Harvest House)

Christ in the Chaos by Kimm Crandall (Cruciform Press)

Grace for the Good Girl by Emily P. Freeman (Revell)

Glimpses of Grace: Treasuring the Gospel in Your Home by Gloria Furman (Crossway)

Bible Study for Children

Exploring Grace Together: 40 Devotionals for the Family by Jessica Thompson (Crossway)

The Jesus Storybook Bible by Sally Lloyd-Jones (Zonderkidz)

Thoughts to Make Your Heart Sing by Sally Lloyd-Jones (Zonderkidz)

Big Truths for Little Kids by Susan Hunt, Richie Hunt, and Nancy Munger (Crossway)

The Gospel Story Bible: Discovering Jesus in the Old and New Testaments by Marty Machowski and A. E. Macha (New Growth Press)

Westminster Shorter Catechism for Kids by Caroline Weerstra (Common Life Press)

Bible Doctrine

Bible Doctrine: Essential Teachings of the Christian Faith by Wayne Grudem and Jeff Purswell (Zondervan)

Pilgrim Theology: Core Doctrines for Christian Disciples by Michael S. Horton (Zondervan)

A Little Book for New Theologians by Kelly M. Kapic (IVP Academic)

Practical Theology for Women by Wendy Horger Alsup (Crossway)

Tough Topics: Biblical Answers to 25 Challenging Questions by Sam Storms (Crossway)

Cross Talk: Where Life and Scripture Meet by Michael Emlet (New Growth Press)

Bible Basics for New Believers by Roy Zuck (Crossway)

On the Grace of God by Justin Holcomb (Crossway)

The Reason for God by Tim Keller (Dutton Adult)

Specific Topics (Related to Chapters in This Book)

Chapter 2: What Is Sin?

Any of the Bible doctrine books above would be helpful in gaining a fuller understanding of sin.

The Heidelberg Catechism: A Study Guide by G. I. Williamson (P & R Publishing)

The Westminster Catechism (Shorter or Larger version)

Christian Beliefs: Twenty Basics Every Christian Should Know by Wayne Grudem (Zondervan)

Respectable Sins: Confronting the Sins We Tolerate by Jerry Bridges (NavPress)

Chapter 3: Why Do People Die?

How Long, O Lord? Reflections on Suffering and Evil by D. A. Carson (Baker)

Suffering and the Sovereignty of God by John Piper (Crossway)

When God Weeps by Joni Eareckson Tada and Steve Estes (Zondervan)

The Problem of Pain by C. S. Lewis (HarperOne)

A Grief Observed by C. S. Lewis (HarperOne)

If God Is Good: Why Do We Hurt? by Randy Alcorn (Multnomah Books)

The Undistracted Widow: Living for God After Losing Your Husband by Carol Cornish (Crossway)

Grief: Finding Hope Again by Paul David Tripp (New Growth Press)

Grieving a Suicide by David Powlison (New Growth Press)

Facing the Death of Someone You Love by Elisabeth Elliot (Crossway)

When Your Family's Lost a Loved One by David and Nancy Guthrie (Tyndale)

Any books or resources by Nancy Guthrie

Chapter 4: Who Is Satan? What Is Hell?

Tough Topics: Biblical Answers to 25 Challenging Questions by Sam Storms (Crossway)

Screwtape Letters by C. S. Lewis (HarperOne)

The Reason for God by Timothy Keller (Dutton Adult)

What Happens After I Die? by Michael Allen Rogers (Crossway)

Chapter 5: Why Do People Get Divorced?

Divorce Care by Steve Grissom and Kathy Leonard (Thomas Nelson)

Marriage, Divorce and Remarriage in the Bible by Jay E. Adams (Zondervan)

Children and Divorce: Helping When Life Interrupts by Amy Baker (New Growth Press)

Divorce Recovery: Growing and Healing God's Way by Winston T. Smith (New Growth Press)

The Meaning of Marriage by Tim and Kathy Keller (Dutton Adult)

Chapter 6: Why Does the Bible Say That? Difficult Bible Stories

How to Read the Bible for All Its Worth by Gordon D. Fee and Douglas Stuart (Zondervan)

The Reason for God by Tim Keller (Dutton Adult)

Amazing Tales and Strange Stories from the Bible by Christopher Doyle (Concordia Publishing)

Icky Sticky, Hairy Scary Bible Stories: 60 Poems for Kids by Jonathan Schkade (Concordia Publishing)

Chapter 7: Why and How Do Some People Sin Sexually?

Washed and Waiting: Reflections on Christian Faithfulness and Homosexuality by Wesley Hill (Zondervan)

The Secret Thoughts of an Unlikely Convert: An English Professor's Journey into Christian Faith by Rosaria Champagne Butterfield (Crown and Covenant Publications)

Rid of My Disgrace: Hope and Healing for Victims of Sexual Assault by Justin and Lindsey Holcomb (Crossway)

Shame Interrupted: How God Lifts the Pain of Worthlessness and Rejection by Edward T. Welch (New Growth Press)

Your Gay Child Says "I Do" edited by R. Nicholas Black (New Growth Press)

How to Talk to Your Kids About Sex by William P. Smith (New Growth Press)

Recovering from Child Abuse by David Powlison (New Growth Press)

Sexual Assault: Healing Steps for Victims by David Powlison (New Growth Press)

What's Wrong With a Little Porn When You're Married/When You're Single? by R. Nicholas Black (New Growth Press)

Chapter 8: Why Does God Let Natural Disasters Happen?

How Long, O Lord? Reflections on Suffering and Evil by D. A. Carson (Baker)

Suffering and the Sovereignty of God by John Piper (Crossway)

When God Weeps by Joni Eareckson Tada and Steve Estes (Zondervan)

The Problem of Pain by C. S. Lewis (HarperOne)

A Grief Observed by C. S. Lewis (HarperOne)

If God Is Good: Why Do We Hurt? by Randy Alcorn (Multnomah Books)

When Bad Things Happen by William P. Smith (New Growth Press)

When Crisis Hits by Jack Miller (New Growth Press)

Chapter 9: Why Do People Fight and Kill?

War of Words: Getting to the Heart of Your Communication Struggles by Paul David Tripp (Resources for Changing Lives)

War, Peace and Christianity: Questions and Answers from a Just-War Perspective by J. Daryl Charles and Timothy J. Bemy (Crossway)

Leaving Your Family Behind: Preparing for Military Deployment by Rob Green (New Growth Press)

Reuniting After Military Deployment by Rob Green (New Growth Press)

Chapter 10: The Good News That Should Always Be Shared

Give Them Grace: Dazzling Your Kids with the Love of Jesus by Elyse Fitzpatrick and Jessica Thompson (Crossway)

Because He Loves Me by Elyse Fitzpatrick (Crossway)

A Gospel Primer by Milton Vincent (Focus Publishing)

The Explicit Gospel by Matt Chandler and Jared Wilson (Crossway)

One Way Love: Inexhaustible Grace for an Exhausted World by Tullian Tchividjian (David C. Cook)

Leading Your Child to Christ by Marty Machowski (New Growth Press)

Acknowledgments

I (Jessica) would like to thank my community at Westview Church, specifically Jesse and Angie Winkler. Thank you, Jesse, for preaching grace every single week and for reminding me over and over that "it is finished." Angie, you are a joy to my heart. Thank you for all of your encouragement.

I thank God for equipping those who have influenced my writing and thinking: Sally Lloyd-Jones, Tim Keller, Tullian Tchividjian, Justin and Lindsey Holcomb, Sam Storms, Wes Hill, Barbara Duguid, Octavius Winslow, Gloria Furman, Trillia Newbell, and Nancy Guthrie.

I thank God for all the sweet relationships he has given me that build me up and make my heart full. To my sweet children: Wesley, Hayden, and Alexandria—I am not sure how I get to be your momma, but I am grateful. To my family: James, Michele, Joel, Ruth, Eowyn, Colin, and Gabe—your love and the laughter you bring into my life is invaluable. To my parents: Mom and Dad—there really aren't words to say how much you have given me; your generosity in every area is evidence that you believe and live the gospel. Mom, you are one of my best friends, you are my sister in Christ, you are my partner in ministry, and I love you. To my dear friends Jami and Annie, who live across the country but are very close to my heart. To my Dropping Keys girls: Kimm, Lori, Rachel, and Lauren—well, you guys are pretty rad.

Thank you, Andy McGuire at Bethany House, for approaching us with the idea for this book. Your help and encouragement throughout the process was needed and is appreciated. Thanks to Erik Wolgemuth. You are one of the most encouraging people I know. I'm grateful for you, brother.

Lastly to my husband, Cody—you are more than I deserve. Your love for our family and for me is such a gift from God. Thank you for supporting me, for encouraging me, and for keeping life normal. The way you release me to write and speak is amazing and a true testament to God's work in your life.

Notes

Chapter 1: Parenting Is More Than Room and Board

1. Tim Hawkins, Twitter post, April 23, 2013, 7:40 a.m., https://twitter.com/timhawkinscomic/status/326707162745294849.

Chapter 2: What Is Sin?

1. *Westminster Shorter Catechism*, Question 14, http://westminstershorter catechism.net/.
2. *ESV Study Bible* note on 2 Corinthians 5:21, emphasis in original (Wheaton, IL: Crossway, 2008), 1560.
3. Reprinted in *Martin Luther's Basic Theological Writings*, ed. Timothy Lull (Minneapolis: Augsburg Fortress, 2005), 48.

Chapter 3: Why Do People Die?

1. "Talking to Children About Death," adapted from the booklet *Caring About Kids* (DHEW Publication No. 79-939), originally produced by the National Institute of Mental Health, www.cc.nih.gov/ccc/patient_education/pepubs/childeath.pdf.
2. Gerry Koocher, "Discussing Death With Children," *The Therapist As Human*, http://kspope.com/therapistas/death.php.

Chapter 4: Who Is Satan? What Is Hell?

1. Sam Storms, *Tough Topics: Biblical Answers to 25 Challenging Questions* (Wheaton, IL: Crossway, 2013), 137.
2. Timothy Keller's gospel summary, from multiple books and sermons.
3. Storms, *Tough Topics*, 143.
4. Ibid., 160.

Chapter 5: Why Do People Get Divorced?

1. McKinley Irvine, "32 Shocking Divorce Statistics," October 30, 2012, www
.mckinleyirvine.com/blog/divorce/32-shocking-divorce-statistics.
2. Ibid.
3. Ibid.
4. Wayne Stocks, "Statistics Related to Children of Divorce," *Divorce Ministry
4 Kids*, August 15, 2011, http://divorceministry4kids.com/2011/statistics-related
-to-children-of-divorce/.
5. Ibid.
6. *ESV Study Bible*, notes on Matthew 19:6 (Wheaton, IL: Standard Bible
Society, 2008), emphasis in original.

Chapter 6: Why Does the Bible Say That? Difficult Bible Stories

1. Sally Lloyd-Jones, *The Jesus Storybook Bible: Every Story Whispers His
Name* (Grand Rapids, MI: Zonderkidz, 2007), 14–17.
2. Bryan Chapell, editor, *ESV Gospel Transformation Bible* (Wheaton, IL:
Crossway, 2013), ix–x. Used by permission.
3. Jerram Barrs, "Understanding Your Teenager's Doubt," *Resurgence,* http://
theresurgence.com/files/pdf/jerram_barrs_2003_understanding_your_teenagers
_doubt.pdf.

Chapter 7: Why and How Do Some People Sin Sexually?

1. Chiara Sabina, Janis Wolak, and David Finkelhor, "The Nature and Dynam-
ics of Internet Pornography Exposure for Youth," *CyberPsychology and Behavior*
11, no. 6 (2008), http://www.unh.edu/ccrc/pdf/CV169.pdf.
2. Justin Holcomb, *On the Grace of God* (Wheaton, IL: Crossway, 2013), 37.
3. In a Q&A at the Veritas Forum at Columbia University in 2008, pastor
Tim Keller had this to say about the question, Does committing homosexual acts
send you to hell?

> "No. First of all heterosexuality does not get you to heaven [laughter], I
> happen to know this, so how in the world can homosexuality send you
> to hell? . . . Jesus talked about greed ten times more than he talked about
> adultery, for example. Now, one of the problems Christians have here . . .
> Let's be nice to Christians: You know when you are committing adultery . . .
> but almost nobody knows when they are greedy. Nobody thinks they are
> greedy. . . . However, the fact of the matter is that the Bible is much harder
> on greed. It's a horrible sin, a terrible sin. Will greed send you to hell? No,
> what sends you to hell is self-righteousness, thinking you can be your own
> savior and lord. What sends you to heaven is getting a connection with
> Christ, because you realize that you are a sinner and you need intervention
> from outside. That's why it is very misleading even to say homosexuality
> is a sin because . . . Yes, of course, homosexuality is a sin, because greed is
> a sin, because all kinds of things are sins, but what most Christians mean
> when they say that and certainly what non-Christians think they hear that
> is, if you are gay you are going to hell for being gay. It is just not true,

absolutely not true." A video of the full conversation is found at www
.youtube.com/watch?v=IZFCB9sduxQ.

4. Recently, though, there has been a wind of change blowing through the
church. Abstinent and former homosexuals have emerged as leaders, writers, and
speakers in the church. There have been several popular blogs calling for the church
to rethink its idea of what a homosexual is and how homosexuals act. There are
many God-fearing, gospel-loving brothers and sisters who struggle with homosexual attraction.

5. "Who Are the Victims?" *Rape, Abuse and Incest National Network*, www
.rainn.org/get-information/statistics/sexual-assault-victims, accessed February
24, 2014.

6. Joe Carter, "9 Things You Should Know About Pornography and the
Brain," *The Gospel Coalition*, http://thegospelcoalition.org/blogs/tgc/2013/05/08/9
-things-you-should-know-about-pornography-and-the-brain/.

Chapter 8: Why Does God Let Natural Disasters Happen?

1. Mati Goldstein, as quoted in "ZAKA Rescues Eight Students in Haiti,"
CBNNews.com, January 17, 2010, http://www.cbn.com/cbnnews/insideisrael/2010
/January/ZAKA-Rescues-Eight-Students-in-Haiti/.

2. Leon Morris, *The Epistle to the Romans* (Grand Rapids, MI: Eerdmans,
1988), 322.

3. J. B. Phillips, *The New Testament in Modern English* (New York: Touchstone,
1998), paraphrase of Romans 8:19.

4. Eugene Peterson, *The Message* (Colorado Springs, CO: NavPress, 2005),
Romans 8:19–21.

5. Public domain.

6. Tim Keller, *The Reason for God* (New York: Dutton, 2008), 32.

Chapter 9: Why Do People Fight and Kill?

1. Leland Ryken, James Wilhoit, and Tremper Longman III, gen. eds., "Stories
of Violence," *Dictionary of Biblical Imagery* (Downers Grove, IL: IVP, 1998), 916.

2. "Family Violence—Facts and Figures," *National Criminal Justice Refer-
ence Service*, September 2012, https://www.ncjrs.gov/spotlight/family_violence
/facts.html.

Chapter 10: The Good News That Should Always Be Shared

1. Octavius Winslow, *Consider Jesus* (Tigard, OR: Monergism Books, 2011),
ebook.

2. John Piper sermon, "Draw Near to the Throne of Grace with Confidence,"
desiringGod.org, September 15, 1996, www.desiringgod.org/resource-library
/sermons/draw-near-to-the-throne-of-grace-with-confidence.

About the Authors

Elyse Fitzpatrick is a retreat and conference speaker, and the author of numerous books on daily living and the Christian life. She has been married for forty years and has three adult children and six grandchildren. She holds a certificate in biblical counseling from CCEF (San Diego) and an MA in biblical counseling from Trinity Theological Seminary.

Jessica Thompson speaks at women's conferences and other events. She is the author of a devotional book for families, *Exploring Grace Together*, and also the coauthor of *Give Them Grace*, written with her mom, Elyse. Jessica has a bachelor's degree in theology. She and her husband have three children—Wesley, Hayden, and Allie—ranging from elementary school to high school.